INCREDIBLE
p a p e r

flying
machines

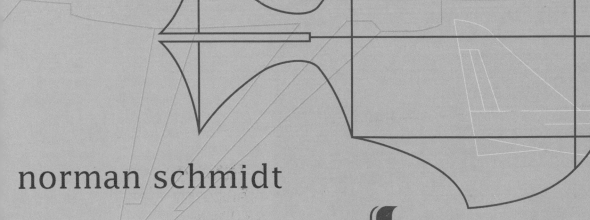

norman schmidt

Sterling Publishing Co., Inc. New York
A Sterling/Tamos Book

A Sterling / Tamos Book
© 2001 Norman Schmidt

First paperback edition published in 2003 by
Sterling Publishing Company, Inc.
387 Park Avenue South, New York, NY 10016

Tamos Books Inc.
300 Wales Avenue, Winnipeg, MB, Canada R2M 2S9

10   9   8   7   6   5   4   3   2   1

Distributed in Canada by Sterling Publishing Co., Inc.
c/o Canadian Manda Group, 1 Atlantic Avenue, Suite 105
Toronto, Ontario, Canada M6K 3E7
Distributed in Great Britain and Europe by Chris Lloyd
at Orca Book Services, Stanley House, Fleets Lane Poole,
BH15 3AJ, England
Distributed in Australia by Capricorn Link (Australia) Pty Ltd.
P.O. Box 704, Windsor, NSW 2756, Australia

Design   Norman Schmidt
Photography   Jerry Grajewski

Printed in China
All rights reserved

CANADIAN CATALOGING IN PUBLICATION DATA

Schmidt, Norman, 1947-

Incredible Paper Flying Machines

"A Sterling/Tamos book."
Includes index.
ISBN 1-895569-37-0 Hardcover
       1-4027-0647-2 Paperback
1. Paper Airplanes.   I. Title.

TL778.S354 2001   745.592   C2001-910634-3

LIBRARY OF CONGRESS
CATALOGING IN PUBLICATION DATA AVAILABLE

ISBN 1-895569-37-0 Hardcover
       1-895569-55-9 Paperback

CONTENTS

Before humans had actually taken to the skies by building machines that could imitate birds and other flying creatures, the idea of flight was truly incredible in both senses of the word: it was beyond belief and wonderful. Air, where flight took place, was invisible and etherial. How it could support machines and creatures made flight seem magical. Human beings wanted to share this mystical experience and from the dawn of history they have been obsessed with the idea of flying. The steps taken from dreaming about flight to actually taking to the skies resulted in some extraordinary inventions. The first steps were faltering, resulting in failure; others pushed flight forward in leaps and bounds until, late in the 19th century, successful human flight became a possibility. Finally in the 20th century, sustained and controlled flight became a reality. Now the resulting variety of aircraft found at today's airports, and their varied capabilities, is itself an incredible accomplishment.

NOTE The proportions of the aircraft represented in this book have been altered in the paper models to suit the paper medium, and they are not in scale to each other. Some of the paper models are fliers, while others are intended for static display only.

SOME BASICS

Flight is all about balance. There are four opposing forces acting on an airplane in exact balance: gravity/lift and thrust/drag. It is important that for flight an airplane's center of gravity lies just ahead of the wing's center of lift (most weight forward). The elevator, rudder, and ailerons are used to keep an airplane straight and level.

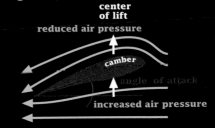

A wing produces lift in two ways as it moves forward. (1) Camber: a curved surface creates a partial vacuum over the wing. (2) Angle of attack: tilting the wing increases pressure beneath the wing. Every wing shape has a correct angle of attack for best performance and beyond a certain angle lift stops (the wing stalls).

center of lift
reduced air pressure
camber
angle of attack
increased air pressure

As an airplane moves forward the wings lift it into the air. To maintain the correct angle of attack the elevator must be angled upward slightly. This is called trimming (adjusting) for cruise. Changing the elevator angle also causes the plane to climb or dive.

lift
center of gravity (balancing point)
elevator pushes tail down
thrust
drag
gravity

An airplane tends to be unstable in three ways. (1) Pitch: the elevator controls the up-and-down movement of the nose. (2) Yaw: the rudder controls its side-to-side movement. (3) Roll: wings are kept level by the ailerons in the wingtips. To adjust (trim) a paper model for straight and level flight simply bend the particular part in the appropriate direction.

(2) rudder
(1) elevator
(3) ailerons

displaying the models

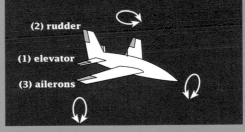

suspend from thread fastened through a small hole pierced at the balancing point

OR

insert into display stand made from a strip of card

To make stand:

mark 4 equal divisions   score

cut (make slit width to fit fuselage thickness)

bend   glue base

general instructions

ALL MODELS

FIRST make photocopies

Make *same-size* photocopies (100%) of the pages containing the pieces for building the paper airplanes.

SECOND prepare guide sheets

Cut the **pieces layout section** from each photocopy, as indicated on the page, to fit a 5 x 8 inch standard index card. Then tack-glue to the card by applying low-tack repositionable glue (e.g Easy Stick Roller) to the backside. Align with the edges of the card.

THIRD advanced planning

Before beginning to cut out the pieces, score those lines (shown in red) that will be needed to bend the piece later, and cut opening slits as needed. Score and cut precisely on the lines.

FOURTH cut out the pieces

Cut out each piece shown. This must be done carefully, since the success or failure of every other step depends on accurately cut pieces.

Cut through both the tacked on guide paper and the card stock underneath. Remove the piece and discard the guide paper. This leaves a clean unmarked aircraft piece, ready for assembly. *Keep track of the pieces by lightly writing the piece number in pencil on the backside of each piece.*

If you have not cut paper with a craft knife, begin by making some practice cuts. In pencil draw some squares, triangles, and circles of various sizes on index card stock and cut them out. For straight cuts use a steel edged ruler to guide the knife; make freehand cuts for curved lines. Always cut by drawing the knife towards you and away from the hand used to hold the paper. Continue to practice until you are comfortable with the tools.

Use a sharp craft knife (e.g. an X-acto knife with a #11 blade) on a suitable cutting surface (e.g. Olfa cutting mat). Practice cutting precisely on the line. Always keep the blade sharp.

NOTE For all the cut-out pieces, the side that faces up for cutting will be outward or upward facing on the finished model. This is important for aesthetic and aerodynamic reasons because of the burr on the edges due to cutting.

NON-FLYING MODELS

FIRST build the main parts

Each model consists of several main parts built up of smaller pieces. Follow the sequence shown in the exploded view for each model. Begin with the number one piece, adding the other smaller pieces on each side to complete the larger part. *Align pieces carefully.* Take note of the bent-over tabs.

Stick glue (e.g. Uhu Color Stic), white craft glue, or wood-type model airplane glue can be used. However, it is easier to manage the drying time and reduce warpage with stick glue.

FIRST TACK-GLUE
PHOTOCOPY OF
THE LAYOUT
SECTION TO
CARD USING
LOW-TACK GLUE
(APPLY TO
BACKSIDE OF
PHOTOCOPY)

THEN SCORE
FOLD LINES AND
CUT ALL
OPENINGS
WITHIN THE
PIECES

FINALLY CUT
OUT EACH
PIECE

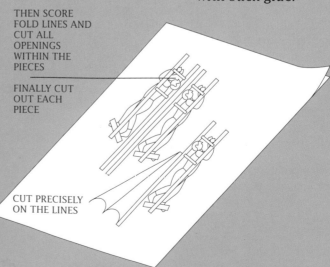

CUT PRECISELY
ON THE LINES

When building up the main parts in layers, apply glue to the entire *smaller* surface to be fastened to a larger one. Press pieces firmly together. Continue until the entire main part is completed.

Lay the assembled parts flat between clean sheets of paper underneath a weight (some heavy books) until the glue is sufficiently set. This will take between 30 and 45 minutes for stick glue, and several hours for white glue.

When the glue is dry add decoration and color to the various main parts of the model before final assembly, if desired.

NOTE If you use felt tipped markers, be sure to use non-toxic ones and work in a well ventilated area.

SECOND put it all together

Apply glue to the various parts or tabs as shown in the instructions for each model. Align parts carefully and press them together to complete the model.

THIRD displaying paper models

For static display, build stands out of index card, or suspend models from a thread, if desired (see p 3). For suspending a model, find the point on the model where it balances and hangs straight and level. Pierce a small hole at this point using a needle. Insert a thread to suspend the model. Models can be suspended independently or they can be assembled into a mobile.

FLYING MODELS

FIRST build fuselage

Build the fuselage following the same procedures described above for building the main parts of the non-fliers.

SECOND wings for flight

Symmetry is essential in wings. Align wing parts carefully. Special care must be taken in those wings consisting of two halves. Temporarily align the halves using masking tape until the joining piece has been glued in place.

On models that require it, the dihedral angle (upward slanting of wings from center to tips) must be adjusted while the parts are being assembled (before the glue is set). Use the angle guide given with the model for details. If stick glue is used, simply prop up the wings at the tips until the glue has set. If white glue (or model glue) is used, drying the wings is complicated. Some means must be devised to keep each wing from warping while maintaining the dihedral angle.

To camber wings, gently massage the paper to give the upper surface a convex curvature.

When the glue is dry add decoration and color to the various main parts of the model before final assembly, if desired.

THIRD put it all together

Apply glue to the bent-over tabs that join the wings and horizontal stabilizer to the fuselage. Align the wings and stabilizers carefully. Press glued parts together. *Adjust placement carefully, viewing the plane from the top, the front, and the back.* **Symmetry and straightness in the completed plane are essential**.

FOURTH camber the wings

This is a critical step. Cambering the wings gives them their ability to generate aerodynamic lift. Holding a wing at the root between thumb and forefinger of both hands, gently massage the paper to give the upper surface a slight convex curvature or camber. Work carefully from the wing root toward the tip and back again. Make sure the left and right wing have the same amount of camber. Avoid kinking the paper. See the instructions for each model for the proper amount of camber.

FIFTH test fly

The paper plane must be well trimmed (adjusted) before it can perform satisfactorily (see p 3).

SIXTH fly for fun

Paper planes perform best out-of-doors in a light breeze in wide-open spaces, away from obstructions and traffic.

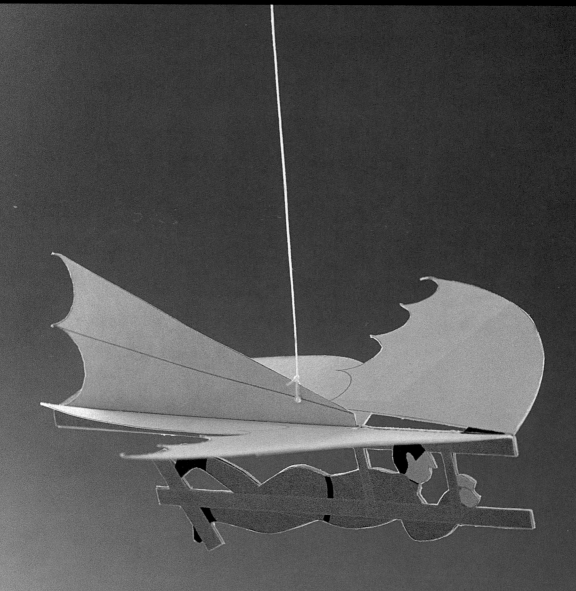

1

Photocopy the layout pages
of pieces for this model.
Then cut out and prepare
the parts for assembly.
(See the general instructions
beginning on p 4.)

2

Bend fastening tabs on
parts 3L and 3R.

Glue part 3L to the bottom
of wing part 4L, aligning
carefully. Repeat, gluing
3R to the bottom of 4R.

3

On the left, glue tab of wing
part 4L to the upper rail of
center part 1C. Repeat on
the right, gluing tab of wing
part 4R to the upper rail of
center part 1C.

4

Glue part 2L to the left
side of center part 1C,
aligning carefully. Repeat
on the right, gluing part
2R to center part 1C.

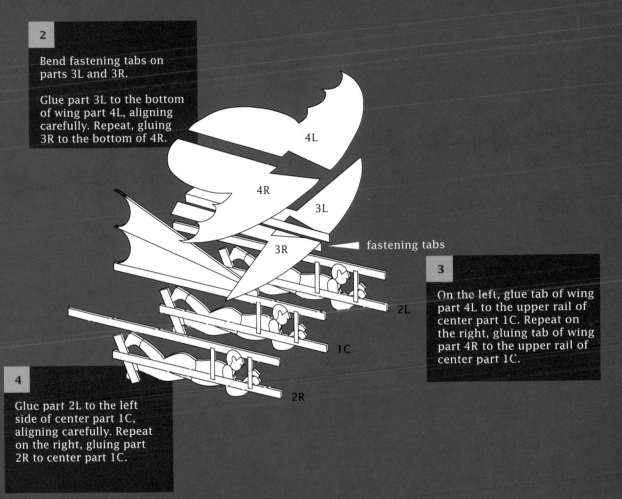

4L

4R

3L

3R

fastening tabs

2L

1C

2R

the finished
aircraft

- Cut on lines shown in black.
- Score lines in red.
- Use the blue lines as guides for adding details to the aircraft.
- ❯ Indicates the front edge of the piece.

CUT OUT PHOTOCOPY ONLY

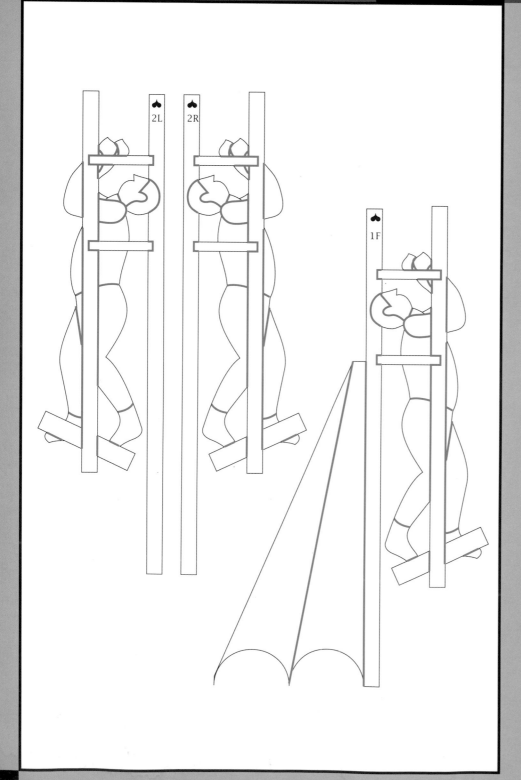

Leonardo da Vinci (1452-1519) was fascinated by many kinds of natural forms, and this led him to make notes and sketches of plants, animals, birds, and human beings, filling nearly 6000 pages. In fact, he was interested in so many things that during his lifetime he worked at painting, sculpture, architecture, engineering, botany, geology, astronomy, anatomy, geography, armament design, and aviation. He was also a musician, singing and performing on instruments of his own invention. His accomplishments were incredible.

Because of his interest in the mechanics of things, Leonardo observed birds in flight, making many sketches of birds' wings in various positions. He thought that the action of birds' wings could be duplicated mechanically in a flying machine powered by a human, much as one peddles a bicycle. He made drawings of various wing-flapping machines (called ornithopters) to be built of wood, with the pilot in a prone or upright position on a ladder-like frame. Peddles were mechanially connected to wings that were made of cloth stretched on a frame.

Unfortunately, the true nature of bird flight was clouded by the fact that birds flap their wings. Flight

LEONARDO PIECES

- Cut on lines shown in black.
- Score lines in red.
- Use the blue lines as guides for adding details to the aircraft.
- ❥ Indicates the front edge of the piece.

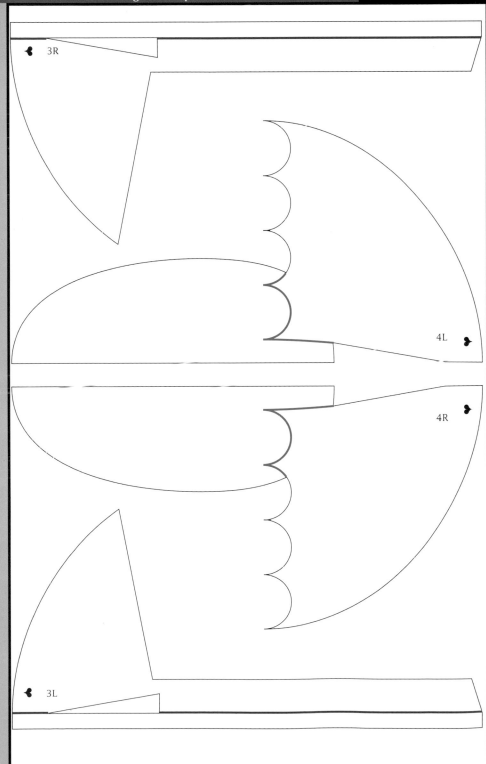

itself has nothing to do with wing flapping but only with the curved shape of the feathers and wings. Moving the wings is used only for propulsion and maneuvering. Once airborne, soaring birds, such as hawks, eagles, and pelicans fly perfectly well without a single wingbeat.

Although Leonardo was aware of the complexity of bird flight and the dual function of wings, his ornithopters don't actually work. People have built them from his plans. He did not have an adequate understanding of the relationship between lift, drag, weight, and power to give his machines the shape and proportions required for flight.

Human powered flight was not achieved until 1977, and then, not with an ornithopter. It was with Paul McGready's scientifically designed propeller-driven and peddle operated airplane, the Gossamer Condor. This machine had huge wings that created lift at a very slow speed and a propeller that turned very slowly. The construction of this craft was possible only because of the existence of very strong ultra-lightweight material. With it human muscle power proved just enough to propel the weight of a human through the air.

2 BEZNIER flapper

1

Photocopy the layout pages of pieces for this model. Then cut out and prepare the parts for assembly. (See the general instructions beginning on p 4.)

4

Bend fastening tabs on wing flap pieces 4L and 5L, gluing them to the front and back ends of the fuselage on the right side.

2

Glue fuselage piece 2L to the left side and 2R to the right side of fuselage piece 1F, aligning carefully.

3

Glue fuselage stiffener 3L to the left side and 3R to the right side of the fuselage, aligning carefully.

5

Bend fastening tabs on wing flap pieces 4R and 5R, gluing them to the front and back ends of the fuselage on the right side.

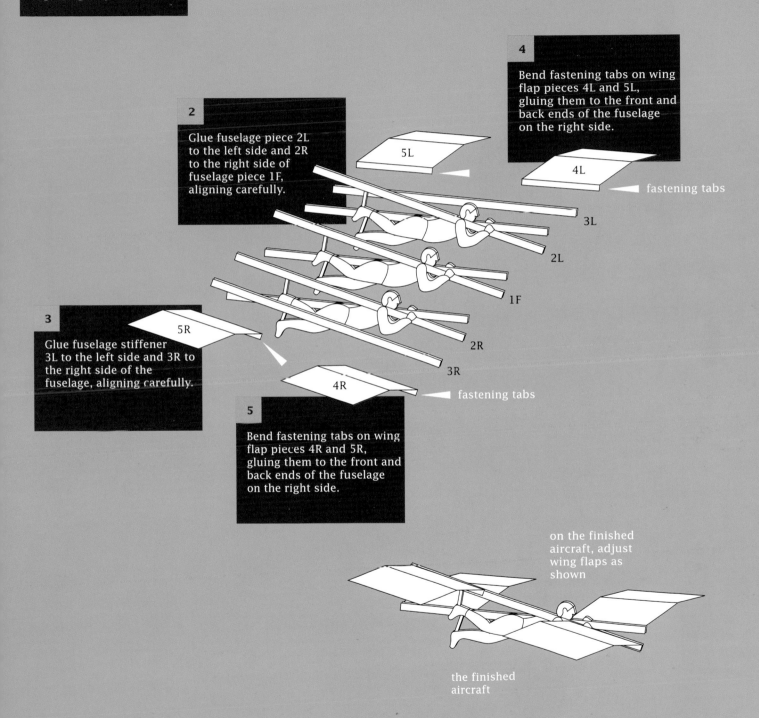

5L

4L

fastening tabs

3L

2L

1F

5R

2R

3R

4R

fastening tabs

on the finished aircraft, adjust wing flaps as shown

the finished aircraft

- Cut on lines shown in black.
- Score lines in red.
- Use the blue lines as guides for adding details to the aircraft.
- ↱ Indicates the front edge of the piece.

CUT OUT PHOTOCOPY ONLY

Incredible as it may seem to us today, for a long time it was thought that simply strapping on some wings, flapping them with arms and legs, while jumping from some high place would result in human flight. There were many of these jumpers and flappers over the centuries. Among them was a French locksmith named Beznier. In 1678 he built a wing-flapping apparatus. His invention differed from most others because he had not only one set of wings, but two. His machine consisted of a pole held over each shoulder with a hinged wing at each end. The poles were attached to his wrists and ankles by ropes. He would then pump his arms and legs up and down. During each upward sweep

BEZNIER PIECES

- Cut on lines shown in black.
- Score lines in red.
- Use the blue lines as guides for adding details to the aircraft.
- ✦ Indicates the front edge of the piece.

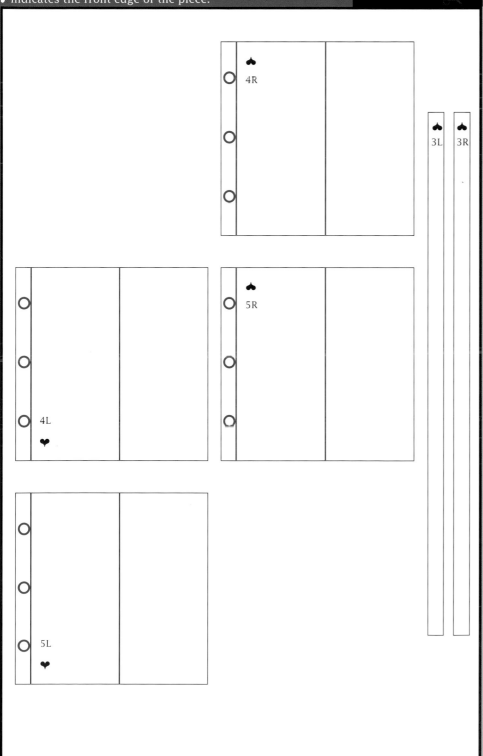

the hinged wings would fold closed, and with each downward sweep they would open flat. Thus one hand wing and the opposite foot wing would always be open while the other two were folded. This alternating up and down, opening and closing motion was intended to provide lift and propulsion. Accounts of his attempts at flight with this apparatus indicate that he could jump from his roof and actually fly across neighboring houses. People were so impressed with the results attained with his machine that he sold an example to a fellow countryman, who, it is said, also had some measure of success.

B CASKEY glider

1

Photocopy the layout pages of pieces for this model. Then cut out and prepare the parts for assembly. (See the general instructions beginning on p 4.)

2

Bend fastening tabs on pieces 8L and 8R.

3

Glue fuselage piece 1F through 8L and 8R to build up fuselage layers, aligning pieces carefully.

4

Glue 10B to the bottom of wing piece 9T, aligning centers. Set dihedral as shown below.

5

Applying glue to the fastening tabs, attach the wing assembly to the fuselage, aligning center lines.

6

Camber the wings by curving the paper gently between thumb and forefinger. See below.

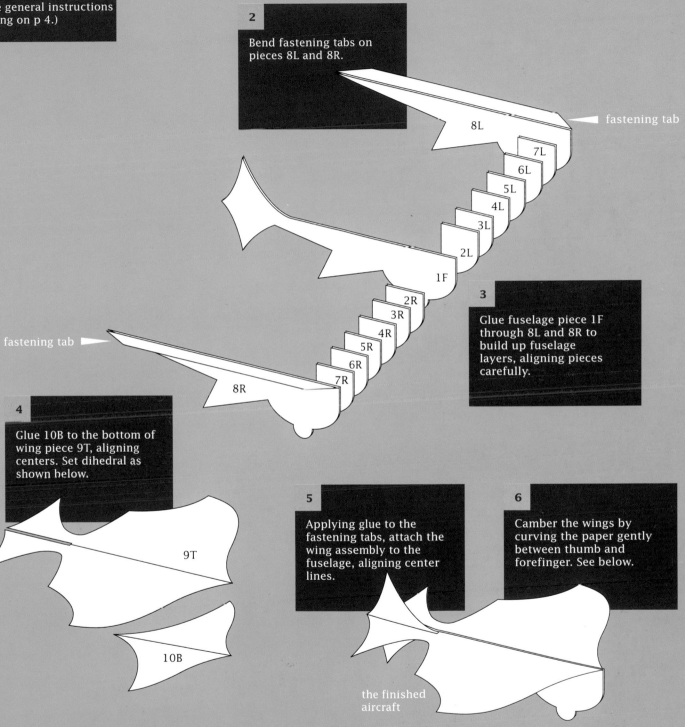

fastening tab

fastening tab

8L
7L
6L
5L
4L
3L
2L
1F
2R
3R
4R
5R
6R
7R
8R

9T

10B

the finished aircraft

dihedral angle: wings 3°

- Cut on lines shown in black.
- Score lines in red.
- Use the blue lines as guides for adding details to the aircraft.
- Indicates the front edge of the piece.

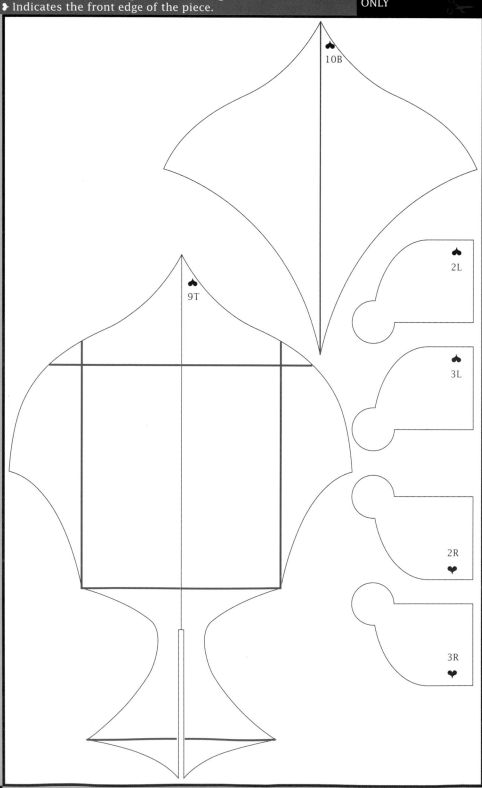

Sir George Cayley was an English aristocrat, who, while still in his twenties, demonstrated a model helicopter built of feathers and bottle corks and a small glider based on kite designs. He worked out mathematical formulae for lift and drag factors and understood the importance of a curved wing surface to create a pressure differential over and under the wing to generate a lifting force. His model glider, built in 1804, already had in place all the correct shapes of the major parts that one might find on airplanes today.

In Cayley's day inventors were experimenting with various kinds of engines for generating power and the most important were steam engines. But these engines were too big and heavy and had only small power output. Cayley realized that they were unsuitable for use in airplanes. Therefore he spent no time on powered flight, concentrating instead on solving the problems of lift and drag in gliding flight.

CAYLEY PIECES

- Cut on lines shown in black.
- Score lines in red.
- Use the blue lines as guides for adding details to the aircraft.
- Indicates the front edge of the piece.

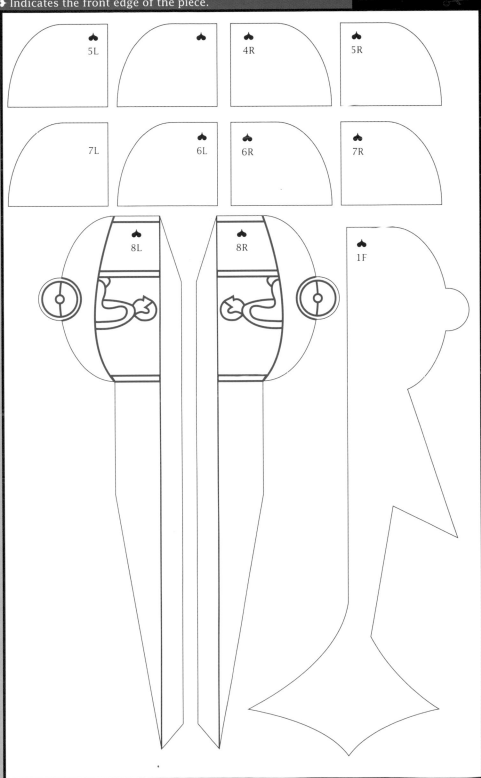

In the 1840s he was working on various designs of full-size gliders. These were kite-like in shape with boat-like fuselages slung underneath. Cayley still had not figured out a means of turning. Gaining confidence from many successful unmanned gliding flights, Cayley, in 1853 persuaded his coachman to climb on board and glide from a high point in a straight descending glide. This has been set down in history as the first observed and recorded free-flight of a human being in a heavier-than-air machine. It earned Cayley the title of Father of Aviation. The coachman, on the other hand, was no aviator, and upon landing handed in his notice, declaring that he had been hired to drive not fly.

4 HENSON
ariel

1

Photocopy the layout pages
of pieces for this model.
Then cut out and prepare
the parts for assembly.
(See the general instructions
beginning on p 4.)

2

Bend fastening tabs on
pieces 4L and 4R.

fastening tab

4L

3L

2L

1F

fastening tab

2R

3

Glue fuselage piece 1F
through 4L and 4R to
build up fuselage
layers, aligning pieces
carefully.

3R

4R

4

Glue 6B to the bottom of
wing piece 5T, aligning
centers. No dihedral.

Glue the two wheel
assemblies 7A through 10D.

glue inside

7A

8B

glue inside

9C

10D

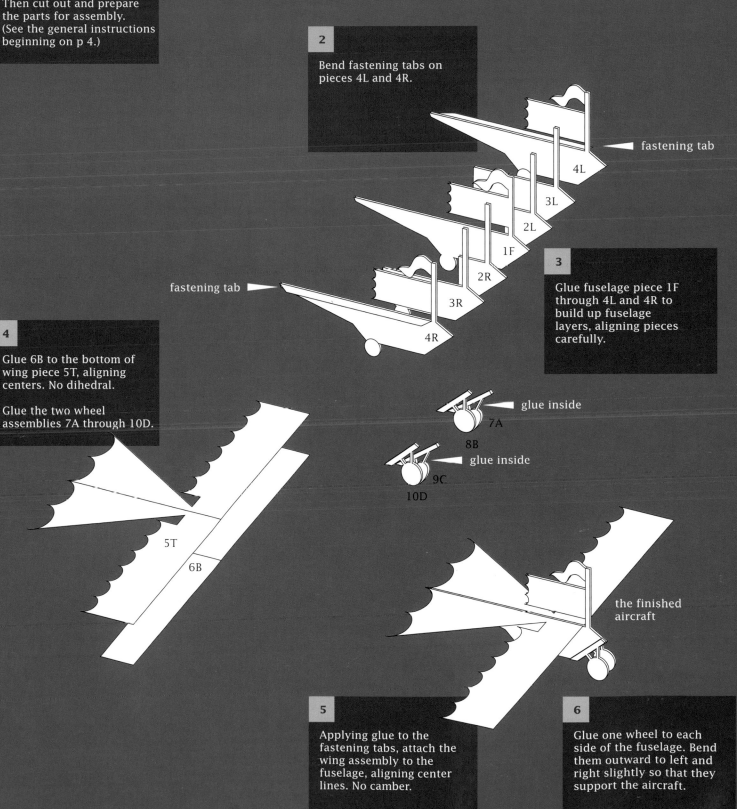

5T

6B

the finished
aircraft

5

Applying glue to the
fastening tabs, attach the
wing assembly to the
fuselage, aligning center
lines. No camber.

6

Glue one wheel to each
side of the fuselage. Bend
them outward to left and
right slightly so that they
support the aircraft.

- Cut on lines shown in black.
- Score lines in red.
- Use the blue lines as guides for adding details to the aircraft.
- Indicates the front edge of the piece.

NOTE
CUT OUT PHOTOCOPY ONLY

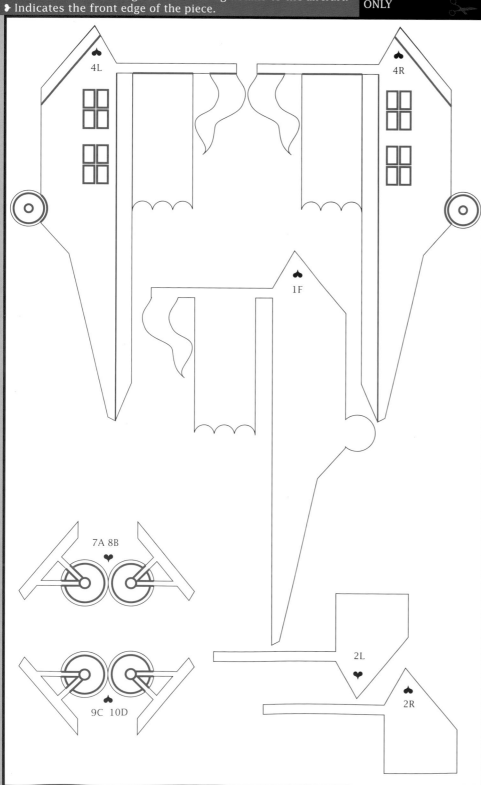

The 19th century was the age of steam power. Steam drove industrial plants, farm machinery, and trains.

William Samuel Henson was a British civil engineer who had followed Cayley's experiments with keen interest. Unlike Cayley, his dream was to build a steam driven airplane, which he called the Ariel Steam Carriage. It was an incredible yet ingenious flying machine. Its design proposed a wingspan of 150 feet (46m) and weight (empty) up to 3000 lb (1400kg). This monoplane had an enclosed fuselage for engine, crew, passengers, and freight, with the entire structure covered in oiled silk.

Henson's design generated a great deal of public interest. In 1843 it even led to the Ariel Transit Bill being introduced in the Britsh

HENSON PIECES

- Cut on lines shown in black.
- Score lines in red.
- Use the blue lines as guides for adding details to the aircraft.
- Indicates the front edge of the piece.

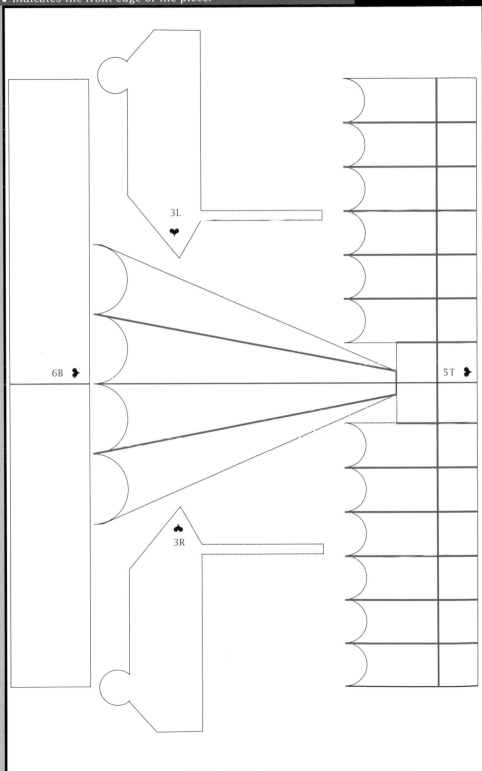

parliament, calling for companies to operate Ariels around the globe. Worldwide publicity pictured Ariels steaming majestically, flags atop the masts, high over town and country – even including the pyramids of Egypt. Atlantic crossings were also planned. Ariel souvenirs were available in plentiful supply.

But Henson's dream, prophetic though it was, far exceeded capability. His 30 hp steam engine could never have driven the machine forward with enough speed for the wings to lift its weight into the air. When even a small lightweight model of the Ariel failed to lift off the ground, plans for its construction were abandoned. Thereafter Henson left Britain, turning his attention to other interests.

Phillips
multiplane

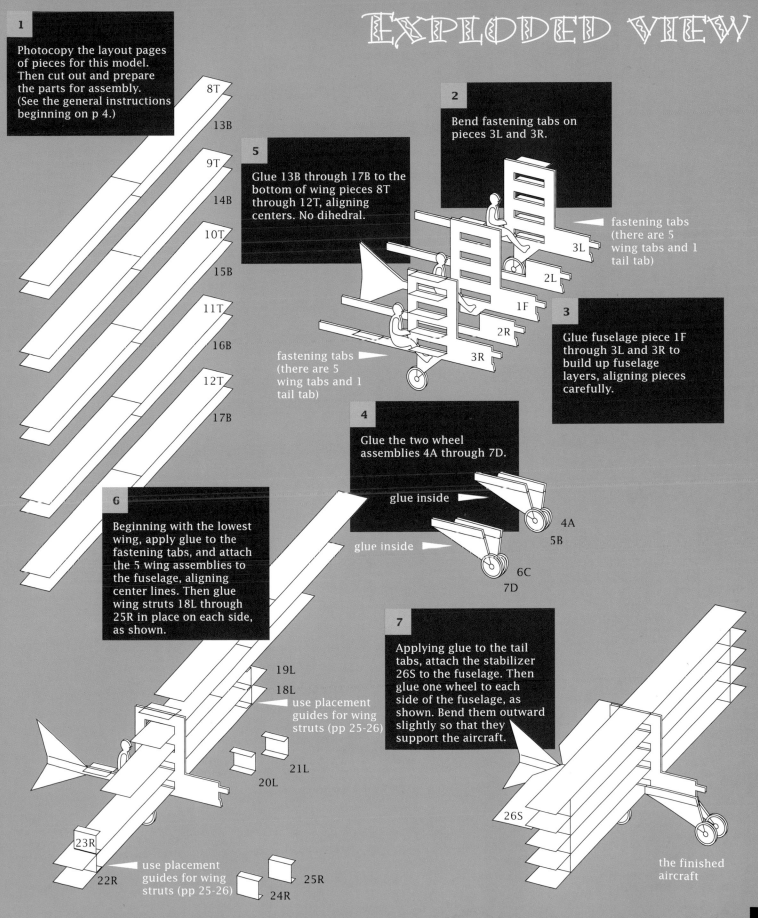

1

Photocopy the layout pages of pieces for this model. Then cut out and prepare the parts for assembly. (See the general instructions beginning on p 4.)

8T

13B

9T

14B

10T

15B

11T

16B

12T

17B

2

Bend fastening tabs on pieces 3L and 3R.

fastening tabs (there are 5 wing tabs and 1 tail tab)

3L

2L

1F

2R

3R

fastening tabs (there are 5 wing tabs and 1 tail tab)

5

Glue 13B through 17B to the bottom of wing pieces 8T through 12T, aligning centers. No dihedral.

3

Glue fuselage piece 1F through 3L and 3R to build up fuselage layers, aligning pieces carefully.

4

Glue the two wheel assemblies 4A through 7D.

glue inside

glue inside

4A

5B

6C

7D

6

Beginning with the lowest wing, apply glue to the fastening tabs, and attach the 5 wing assemblies to the fuselage, aligning center lines. Then glue wing struts 18L through 25R in place on each side, as shown.

19L

18L

use placement guides for wing struts (pp 25-26)

21L

20L

23R

use placement guides for wing struts (pp 25-26)

22R

25R

24R

7

Applying glue to the tail tabs, attach the stabilizer 26S to the fuselage. Then glue one wheel to each side of the fuselage, as shown. Bend them outward slightly so that they support the aircraft.

26S

the finished aircraft

phillips

- Cut on lines shown in black.
- Score lines in red.
- Use the blue lines as guides for adding details to the aircraft.
- ➔ Indicates the front edge of the piece.

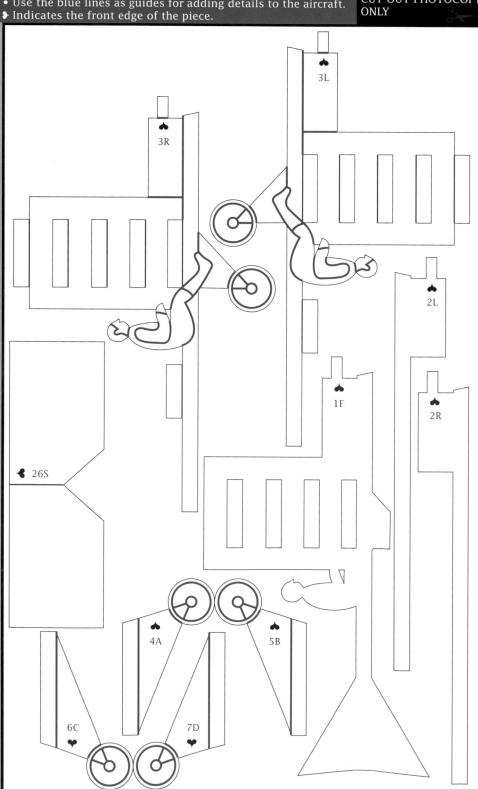

When it became commonly known that the curvature of a wing's upper surface was the key to generating a lifting force, various individuals interpreted its application differently.

Englishman Horatio Phillips experimented with wings of different aspect ratios (proportions of width to length) and discovered that long narrow wings were more efficient in generating lift.

Beginning in 1893 and for many years thereafter, he designed a number of incredible multiplanes. He believed that successful flight could be achieved by stacking many long and narrow wings (high aspect ratio). One of his airplanes had no fewer than 160 such wings, making it look much like a flying venetian blind.

PHILLIPS PIECES

• Cut on lines shown in black.
• Score lines in red.
• Use the blue lines as guides for adding details to the aircraft.
❧ Indicates the front edge of the piece.

WING STRUT
PLACEMENT
GUIDES

8T ❧

9T ❧

10T ❧

11T ❧

12T ❧

WING STRUT
PLACEMENT
GUIDES

Such complex structures were incredibly difficult to support, resulting in many failures during flight trials. For safety's sake many of these were unmanned. No great success resulted from any of the flights. The multiplane's longest flight – unmanned in 1907 – was only about 500 feet (150m).

Phillips is best remembered for his work in experimenting with curved wing surfaces and this influenced the work of others in making the modern high aspect ratio airfoil early in the 20th century. Today gliders have very efficient narrow and long wings allowing them to travel great distances with a minimum loss in altitude.

PHILLIPS PIECES

- Cut on lines shown in black.
- Score lines in red.
- Use the blue lines as guides for adding details to the aircraft.
- ❥ Indicates the front edge of the piece.

18L

19L

20L

21L

22R

23R

24R

25R

17B ❥

16B ❥

15B ❥

14B ❥

13B ❥

WING STRUT
PLACEMENT
GUIDES

WING STRUT
PLACEMENT
GUIDES

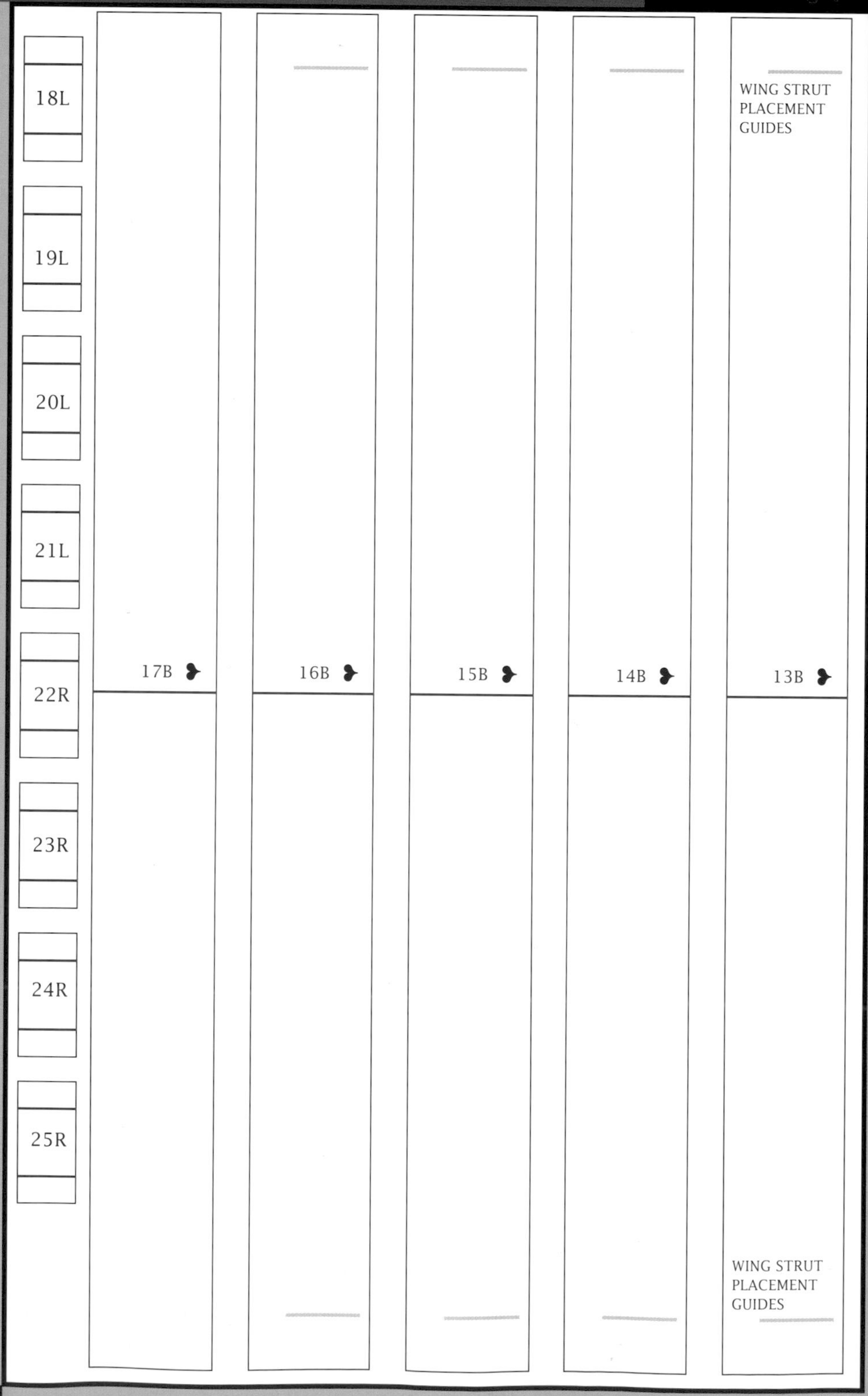

LANGLEY tandem wings

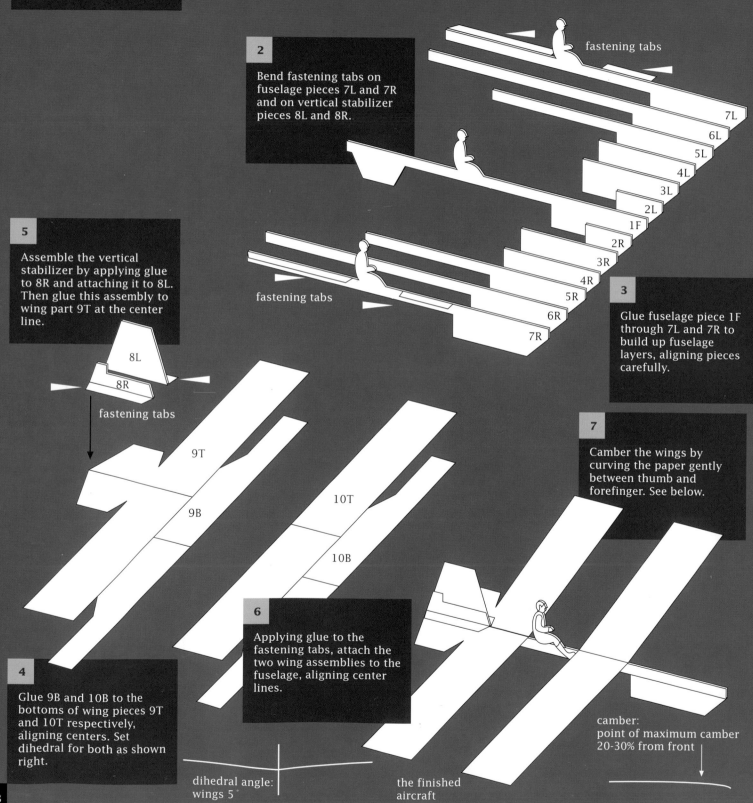

1

Photocopy the layout pages of pieces for this model. Then cut out and prepare the parts for assembly. (See the general instructions beginning on p 4.)

2

Bend fastening tabs on fuselage pieces 7L and 7R and on vertical stabilizer pieces 8L and 8R.

fastening tabs

7L
6L
5L
4L
3L
2L
1F
2R
3R
4R
5R
6R
7R

fastening tabs

3

Glue fuselage piece 1F through 7L and 7R to build up fuselage layers, aligning pieces carefully.

5

Assemble the vertical stabilizer by applying glue to 8R and attaching it to 8L. Then glue this assembly to wing part 9T at the center line.

8L
8R

fastening tabs

9T
9B

10T
10B

7

Camber the wings by curving the paper gently between thumb and forefinger. See below.

6

Applying glue to the fastening tabs, attach the two wing assemblies to the fuselage, aligning center lines.

4

Glue 9B and 10B to the bottoms of wing pieces 9T and 10T respectively, aligning centers. Set dihedral for both as shown right.

dihedral angle: wings 5°

the finished aircraft

camber: point of maximum camber 20-30% from front

THE PIECES

langley

- Cut on lines shown in black.
- Score lines in red.
- Use the blue lines as guides for adding details to the aircraft.
- ❯ Indicates the front edge of the piece.

NOTE
CUT OUT PHOTOCOPY ONLY

The work of professor Samuel Pierpont Langley, secretary of the Smithsonian Institute, is overshadowed by the tremendous success and publicity of the Wright brothers. Consequently Langley's accomplishments are not well known. However he had some incredible achievements in unmanned flight and lost out to the Wrights in the first manned and powered flight only because of some unfortunate mishaps at the wrong time.

In 1891 Langley began building small-scale airplane models. In all of his early experiments he used small steam engines for propul-

LANGLEY PIECES

- Cut on lines shown in black.
- Score lines in red.
- Use the blue lines as guides for adding details to the aircraft.
- ❧ Indicates the front edge of the piece.

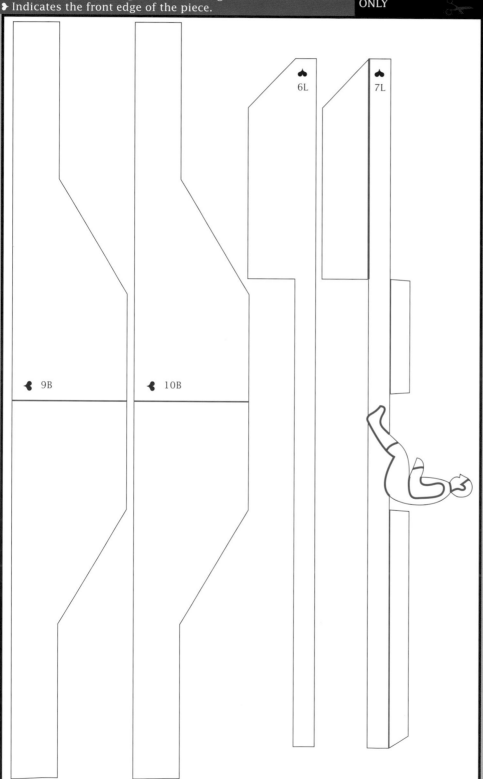

sion. He encountered the same difficulties that all other would-be aviators faced as they attempted to build a frame sufficiently light in weight yet strong enough to withstand the forces of launching and flight. Wing distortion was a major problem. Langley's planes were a tandem wing design – two similar wings mounted one in front of the other, called aerodromes. In 1895, his 14 foot (4m) model airplane managed two flights and utilized a small 1 hp steam engine. Incredibly, the longest flight was over 4000 feet (1200m). Langley was satisfied with these results yet he knew that no steam engine could be built that was light enough with sufficient power to propel a full-

LANGLEY PIECES

- Cut on lines shown in black.
- Score lines in red.
- Use the blue lines as guides for adding details to the aircraft.
- ➧ Indicates the front edge of the piece.

NOTE:
CUT OUT PHOTOCOPY ONLY

4L
5L
9T
10T
8R
8L

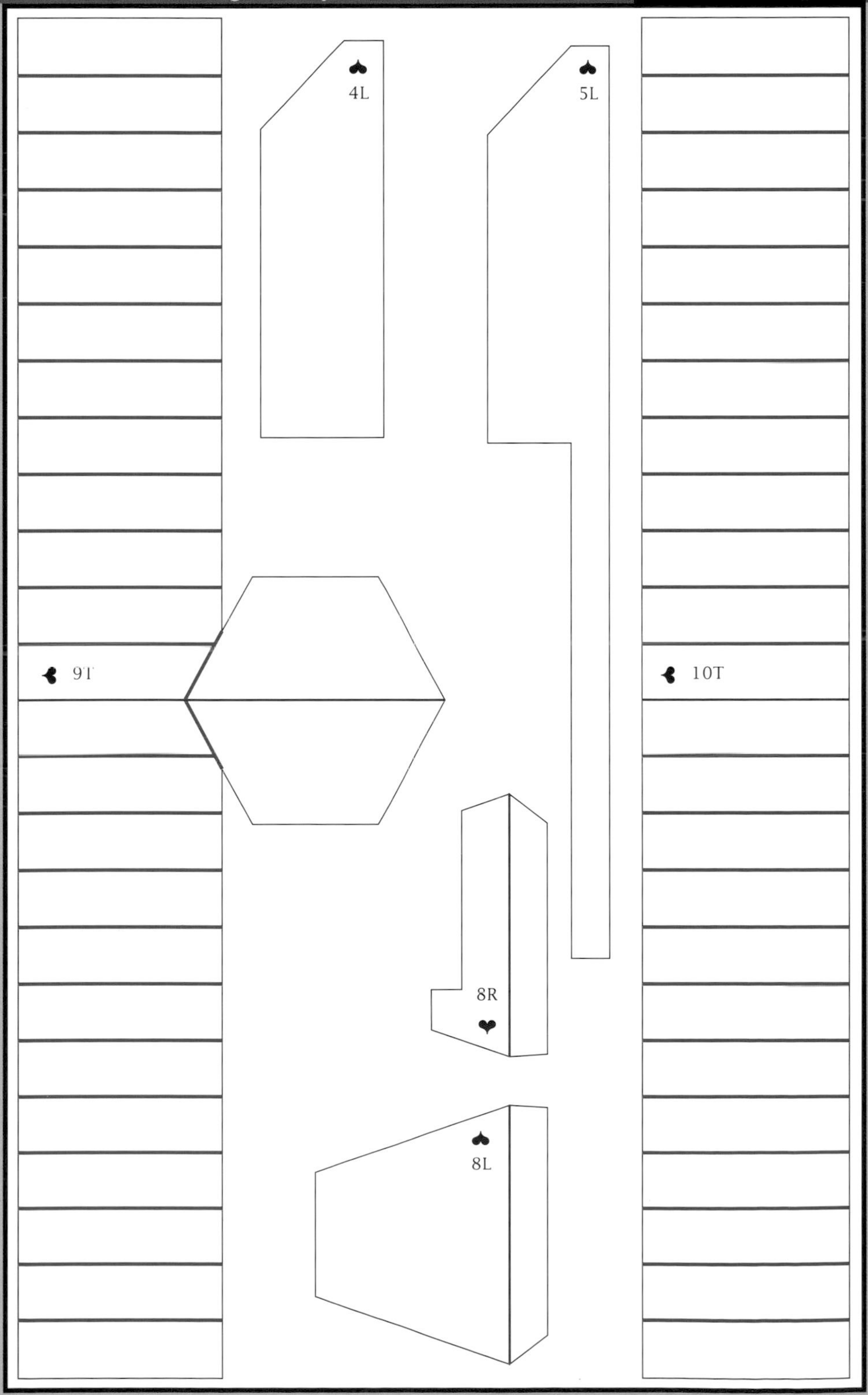

sized airplane. The internal combustion engine had just been invented, and Langley used a 52 hp gasoline-burning radial engine for his larger planes.

An unmanned three-quarter scale model flew well in 1903, the same year that the Wrights had their successful first flight. Unfortunately for Langley, in two attempts, his full-size plane caught the launcher and failed to get airborne. Disappointed, his financial backers withdrew their support for further experimentation. In 1914, long after Langley's death, to prove the merits of the design, his full-size airodrome was rebuilt and flown successfully.

TAYLOR
aerocar

non-flying model
(will fly with wheels removed)

1

Photocopy the layout pages of pieces for this model. Then cut out and prepare the parts for assembly. (See the general instructions beginning on p 4.)

2

Bend fastening tabs on pieces 8L and 7R, including the two wheel tabs.

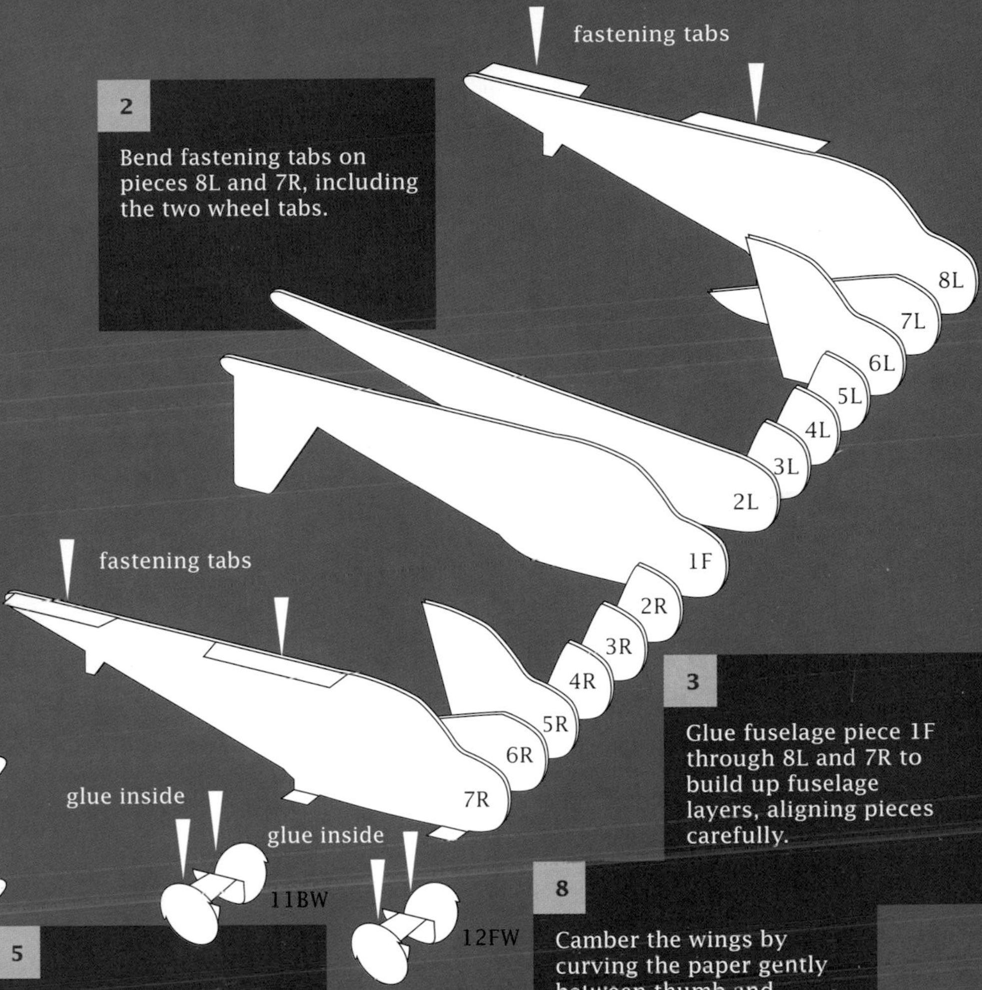

fastening tabs

8L
7L
6L
5L
4L
3L
2L
1F
2R
3R
4R
5R
6R
7R

3

Glue fuselage piece 1F through 8L and 7R to build up fuselage layers, aligning pieces carefully.

fastening tabs

4

Glue 10B to the bottom of wing piece 9T, aligning centers. Set dihedral as shown below.

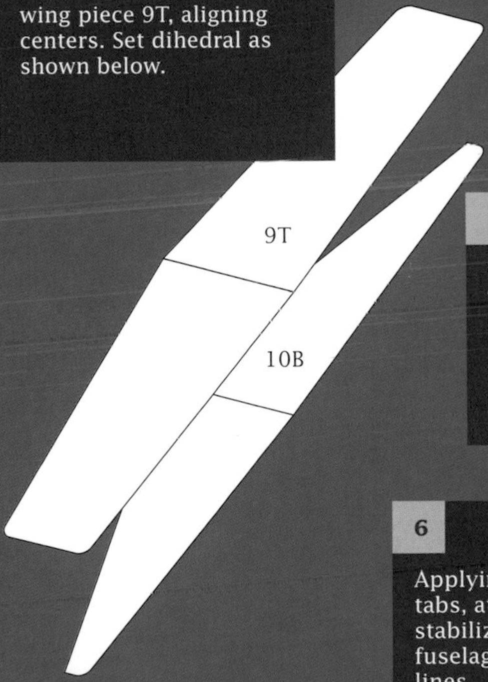

glue inside

glue inside

11BW

12FW

9T

10B

5

Bend, then glue the two wheel assemblies 11BW and 12FW, as shown.

8

Camber the wings by curving the paper gently between thumb and forefinger. See below.

6

Applying glue to the tail tabs, attach the horizontal stabilizer 13S to the fuselage, aligning center lines.

13S

7

Applying glue to the fastening tabs, attach the wing assembly to the fuselage, aligning center lines. Then glue wheel assembly 11BW to the back and 12FW to the front, as shown right.

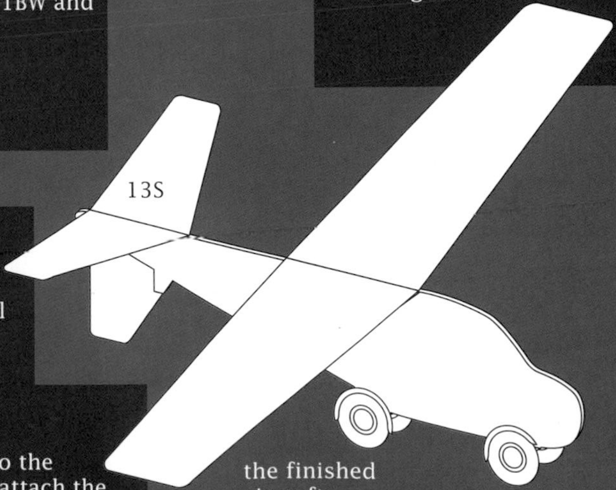

the finished aircraft

dihedral angle:
wings 3°
hor stab 30°

camber:
point of maximum camber 20-30% from front

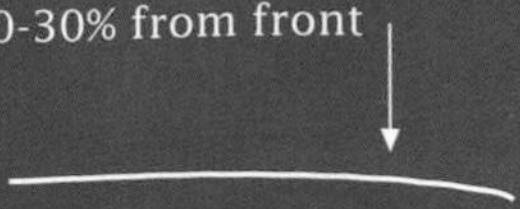

THE PIECES

taylor

• Cut on lines shown in black.
• Score lines in red.
• Use the blue lines as guides for adding details to the aircraft.
❥ Indicates the front edge of the piece.

CUT OUT PHOTOCOPY ONLY

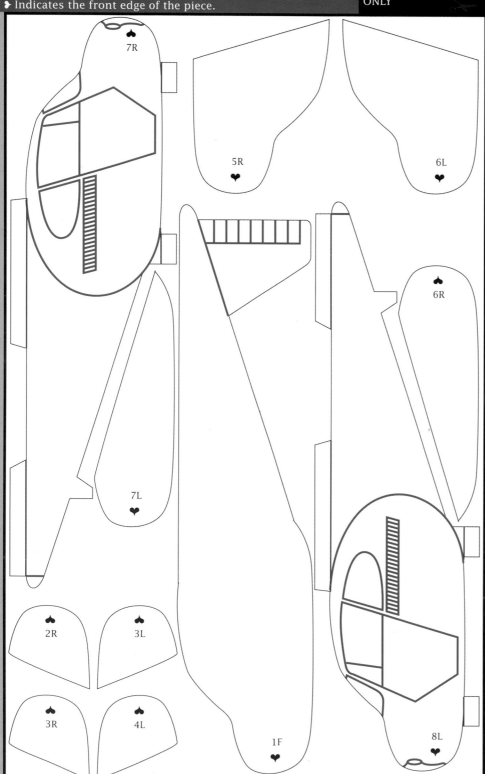

Moulton Taylor was an innovator. During the Second World War he worked for the United States Navy as an aeronautical engineer. He was interested in remotely controlled aircraft, and he was the first to show that an unmanned weapon could change its course after launch. The work he began at that time later became the Tomahawk Missile Program.

After the war another idea captured Taylor's imagination. Since aviation began there were those who dreamed of combining the airplane and the car into a single vehicle that could be flown to some destination and then driven on the ground from that point on. By 1949 Taylor had completed a prototype flying car – the Aerocar.

Some people thought that simply adding wings and tail to a regular car might work. But the problem with ground vehicles is that they are built boxy and heavy to with-

TAYLOR PIECES

- Cut on lines shown in black.
- Score lines in red.
- Use the blue lines as guides for adding details to the aircraft.
- Indicates the front edge of the piece.

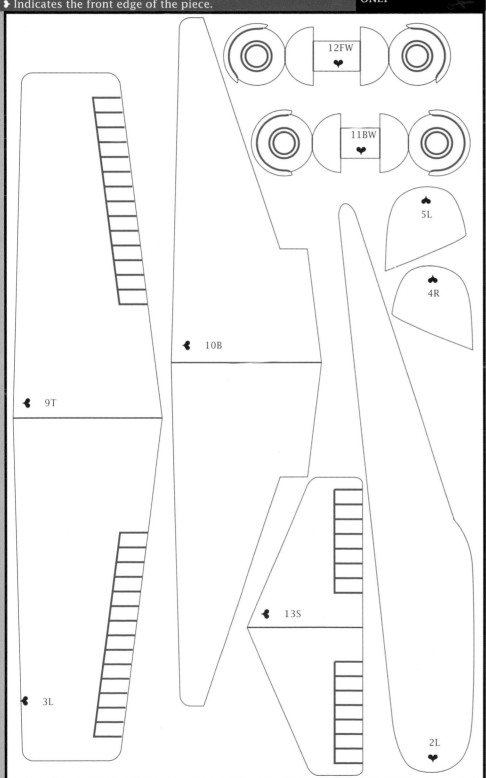

stand traveling over rough roads. Such a vehicle would require a powerful second engine to propel it through the air. Taylor's idea was to first custom build a compact and streamlined automobile using lightweight aircraft materials. This car would have detachable wings and tail which could be loaded on a trailer and towed behing the car while traveling on the ground. The same engine would power the vehicle in the air and on the ground.

While this was a fascinating idea, the work involved in converting from one mode of travel to the other made it impractical for all except the enthusiast. Only a small number of these vehicles were ever built and Taylor's dream of an Aerocar in every garage never happened. However, modern innovators have been inspired by the Aerocar, and today others have taken up the challenge to perfect such a vehicle.

BEDE
BD-5 J micro

1

Photocopy the layout pages
of pieces for this model.
Then cut out and prepare
the parts for assembly.
(See the general instructions
beginning on p 4.)

2

Bend fastening tabs on
pieces 6L, 7L, 6R, and 7R.

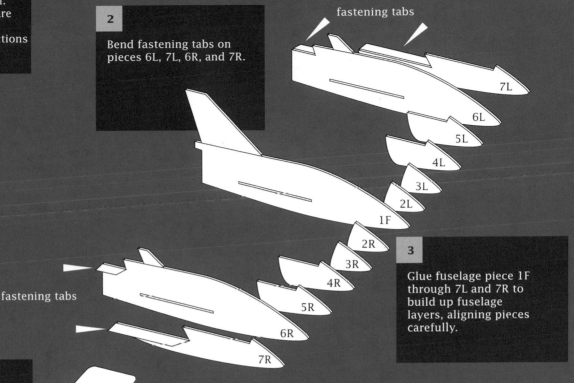

fastening tabs

7L

6L

5L

4L

3L

2L

1F

2R

3R

4R

5R

6R

7R

fastening tabs

3

Glue fuselage piece 1F
through 7L and 7R to
build up fuselage
layers, aligning pieces
carefully.

4

Glue 9B to the bottom of
wing piece 8T, aligning
centers. Set dihedral as
shown below.

8T

9B

5

Applying glue to the
fastening tabs, attach
horizontal stabilizer 10S
and the wing assembly to
the fuselage, as shown,
aligning center lines.

10S

the finished
aircraft

6

Camber the wings by
curving the paper gently
between thumb and
forefinger. See below.

camber:
point of maximum camber
20-30% from front

dihedral angle:
wings 5°

THE PIECES

bede

- Cut on lines shown in black.
- Score lines in red.
- Use the blue lines as guides for adding details to the aircraft.
- ➤ Indicates the front edge of the piece.

NOTE
CUT OUT PHOTOCOPY ONLY

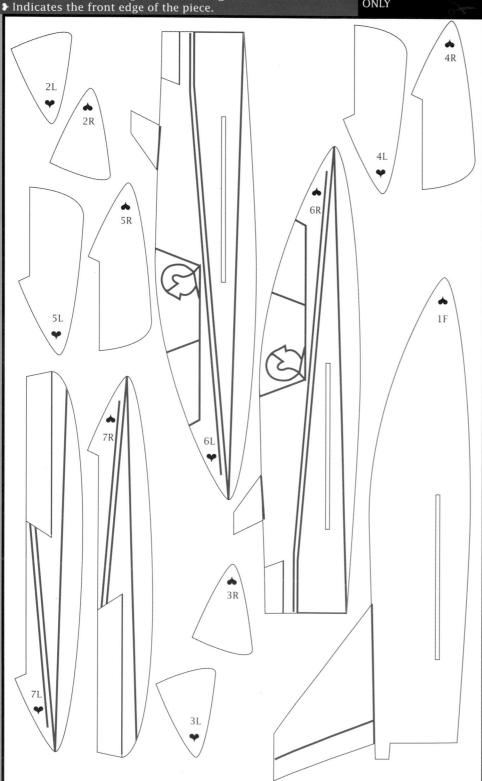

Jim Bede began work on a microsize aircraft in 1967. His imagination was fired by the idea of a low-cost easy-to-build personal sport airplane. The home building of aircraft was just beginning at that time because manufacturers of light airplanes faced ever greater costs and the prices of their airplanes rose to the point of being out of reach for the average private pilot. Since then many light sport aircraft are homebuilt from kits, much like model airplanes, with major components pre-made. But the making of the kit for sale requires a great deal of time and effort in order that the end product will be an airworthy aircraft. Bede was a thorough designer and proceeded with a rigorous test program for the BD-5. Unfortunately, things did not go well.

From the outset there were problems of one kind or another, ranging from stability, to the construction of the airframe, to the

BEDE PIECES

- Cut on lines shown in black.
- Score lines in red.
- Use the blue lines as guides for adding details to the aircraft.
- ❥ Indicates the front edge of the piece.

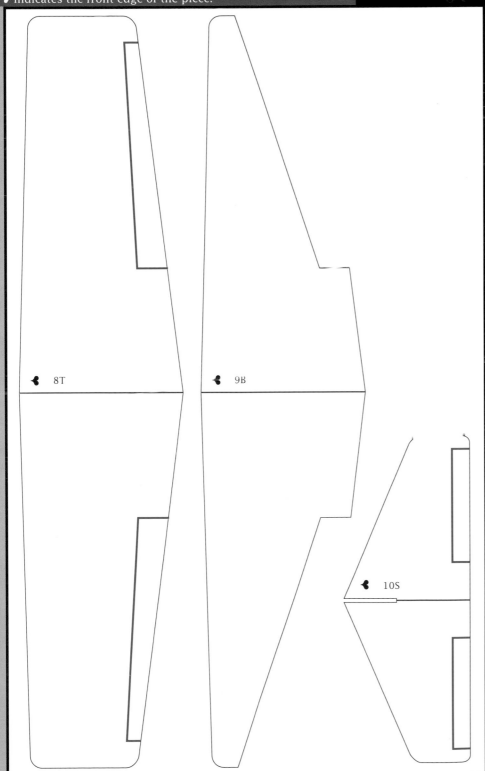

performance of the engine. Many changes to the original design were called for – instead of composites, metal was used for the airframe; instead of a V-tail, a conventional tail was used. Numerous other changes were made as well. All this took years to solve, and early enthusiasts turned to skeptics. Yet while this was going on Bede was working on a more ambitious project – a jet powered version of this micro, the BD-5 J.

The dream of a sky full of BD-5s never happened, yet this incredible little plane still stirs the blood of aviation enthusiasts and a mystique has formed around this machine. Adding to its popularity was the appearance of a fantasized version of the jet in the 1983 James Bond movie *Octopussy*. Those who have flown the BD-5 say that, although not for the fainthearted, it is a fine machine requiring skill and precision to fly.

Montgolfier
balloon

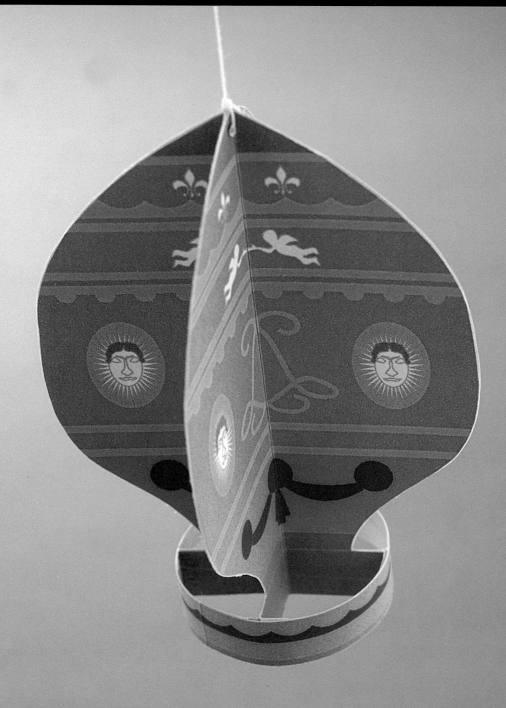

1

Photocopy the layout pages of pieces for this model. Then cut out and prepare the parts for assembly. (See the general instructions beginning on p 4.)

2

Bend pieces 1A through 4D along center lines, as shown. Then bend all the fastening tabs.

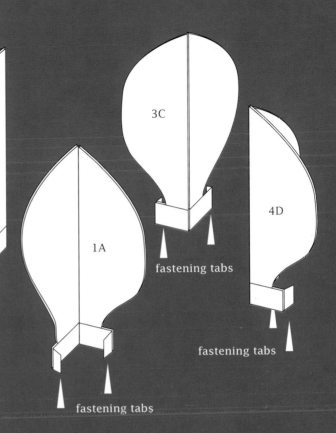

2B

3C

1A

4D

fastening tabs

fastening tabs

fastening tabs

fastening tabs

3

Glue pieces 1A through 4D together to make the main balloon assembly, as shown. Align edges carefully.

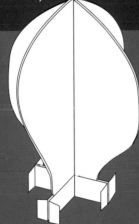

the finished aircraft

5E

wrap around and glue all tabs

4

Applying glue to the fastening tabs on the main assembly and on the joining strip 5E, wrap strip around the base of the main assembly to finish the model balloon.

THE PIECES

montgolfier

- Cut on lines shown in black.
- Score lines in red.
- Use the blue lines as guides for adding details to the aircraft.
- ➤ Indicates the front edge of the piece.

CUT OUT PHOTOCOPY ONLY

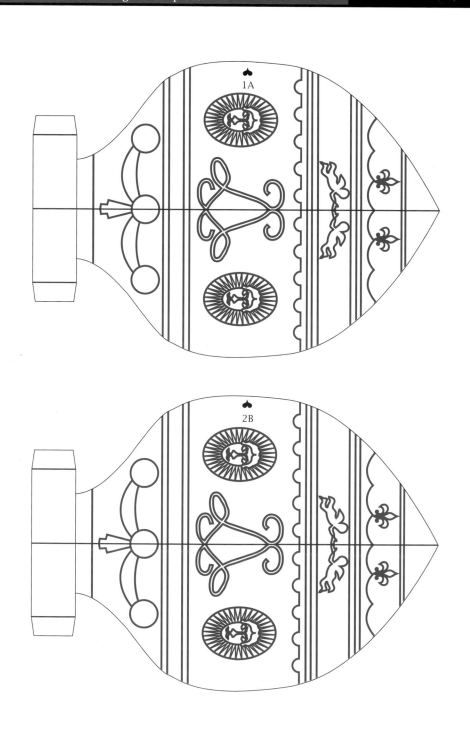

Frenchman Joseph Mont-golfier observed that soot and embers floated up in the smoke of an open fire. He also noticed that a shirt left to dry near an open fire billowed out from the rising smoke. This led him, in 1782, to experiment holding a cloth bag over a fire in an attempt to make it rise. To his delight it lifted sky-ward.

Secretly he and his brother Jacque experimented with larger and larger bags. After about a year they built a large balloon that they calculated could lift more than 400 pounds (200 kg). A straw fire was built beneath it and upon release the balloon rose smoothly to about 1000 feet (300m) and floated across several fields before land-ing. Only after this success were they ready to disclose their work.

In the autumn of 1783 they were asked to demonstrate their inven-tion before the king and queen of France. For this occasion they built

42

MONTGOLFIER PIECES

- Cut on lines shown in black.
- Score lines in red.
- Use the blue lines as guides for adding details to the aircraft.
- Indicates the front edge of the piece.

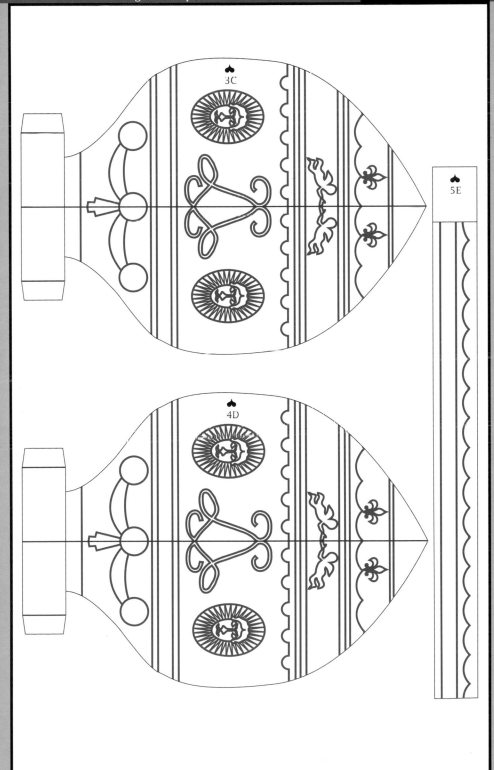

a brightly decorated balloon that measured 41 feet (13 m) in diameter. A wicker cage was suspended beneath the balloon and a sheep, a rooster, and a duck were put inside. The flight, staged at the palace of Versailles, lasted eight minutes and these animals became the first living creatures to fly in a balloon. Some time later François de Rozier climbed aboard and became airborne, but for saftey's sake the balloon remained tethered for this flight.

A month later, however, Rozier and the Marquis d'Arlandes made the first untethered human flight in a larger and more strongly built balloon. The 49 foot (15 m) balloon had a wicker gallery around its base and a brazier for prolonging the flight, When the fire was lit the balloon rose gently, drifting across the city of Paris high over the heads of jubilant crowds and landing 25 minutes later. Within a year balloon ascents had taken place in several other countries.

10 GREAT dirigible

1

Photocopy the layout pages
of pieces for this model.
Then cut out and prepare
the parts for assembly.
(See the general instructions
beginning on p 4.)

2

Bend pieces 1L through 4R
along center lines, as
shown.

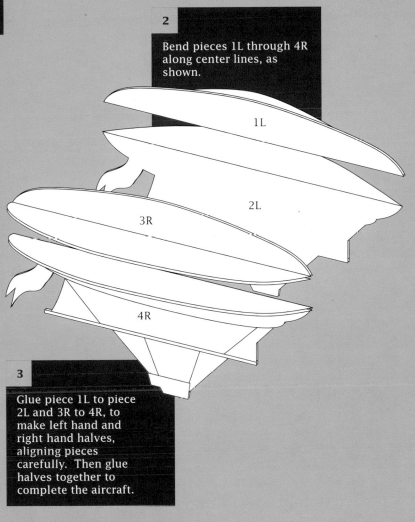

1L

2L

3R

4R

3

Glue piece 1L to piece
2L and 3R to 4R, to
make left hand and
right hand halves,
aligning pieces
carefully. Then glue
halves together to
complete the aircraft.

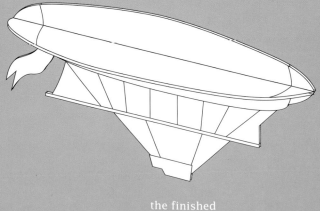

the finished
aircraft

- Cut on lines shown in black.
- Score lines in red.
- Use the blue lines as guides for adding details to the aircraft.
- Indicates the front edge of the piece.

CUT OUT PHOTOCOPY ONLY

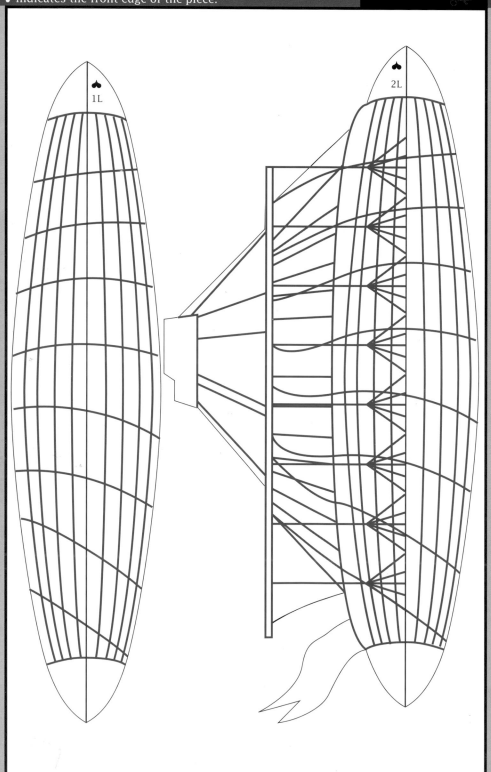

Hot air balloons, although large in size, were relatively simple machines. They were limited in their usefulness, however, because they depended entirely on wind for travel across country. As well as hot air balloons, hydrogen filled balloons were also being made. These were lighter than air and floated of their own accord, but required a more complicated arrangement of two bags, one inside the other for both hydrogen and compressed air, not to mention water ballast. In 1784 an attempt was made to fit a manually-turned propeller to a hydrogen balloon to make a dirigible – a steerable propelled airship. At first this proved unsuccessful. The size was incredible. One of these dirigibles would have required a crew of 80 individuals just to man the propellers and sails.

Over the years different shapes and sizes of airships were made

GIFFARD PIECES

- Cut on lines shown in black.
- Score lines in red.
- Use the blue lines as guides for adding details to the aircraft.
- ➤ Indicates the front edge of the piece.

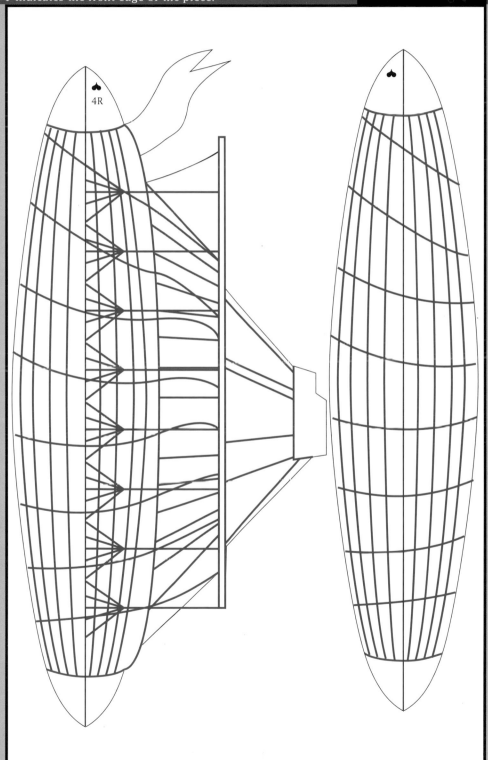

and in 1852 Frenchman Henri Giffard successfully flew a 144 foot (44 m) lozenge-shaped and hydrogen-filled airship propelled by a 3 horsepower steam engine. His dirigible had a flexible gas envelope covered in a rope shroud with the engine and occupants suspended in a gondola underneath. This arrangement of gas envelope above and gondola for crew and passengers beneath became the standard for all future airships.

Traveling at a speed of 5 miles per hour (8 kph) Giffard navigated a course of about 17 miles (27 km), which was the first successful manned, powered, and controlled flight. Incredibly, this was one year before Cayley's coachman made the first successful straight ahead short glide in a heavier-than-air winged aircraft. Giffard's flight set the course for many years of experiments with lighter-than-air flight that rivaled the airplane.

non-flying model

airship

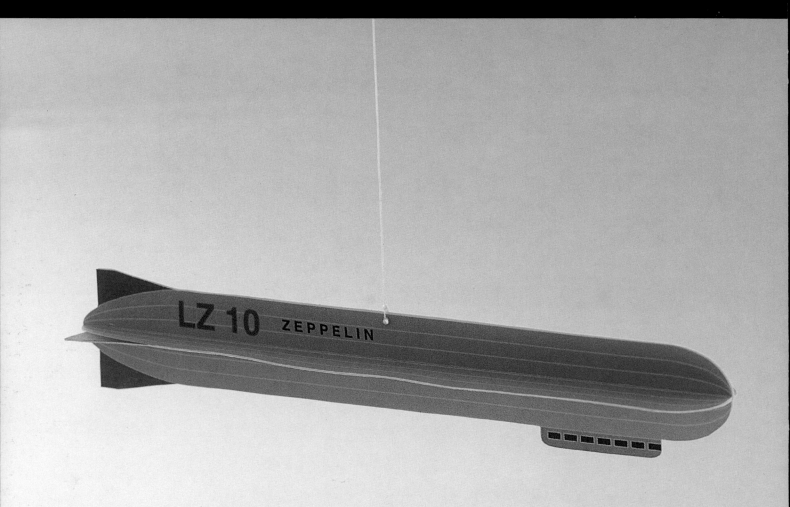

LZ 10 ZEPPELIN

INCREDIBLE SIZE

EXPLODED VIEW

1

Photocopy the layout pages of pieces for this model. Then cut out and prepare the parts for assembly. (See the general instructions beginning on p 4.)

2

Bend pieces 1L through 4R along center lines, as shown.

1L

2L

3R

4R

3

Glue piece 1L to piece 2L and 3R to 4R, to make left hand and right hand halves, aligning pieces carefully. Then glue halves together to complete the aircraft.

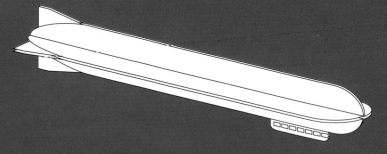

the finished aircraft

- Cut on lines shown in black.
- Score lines in red.
- Use the blue lines as guides for adding details to the aircraft.
- Indicates the front edge of the piece.

NOTE
CUT OUT PHOTOCOPY
ONLY

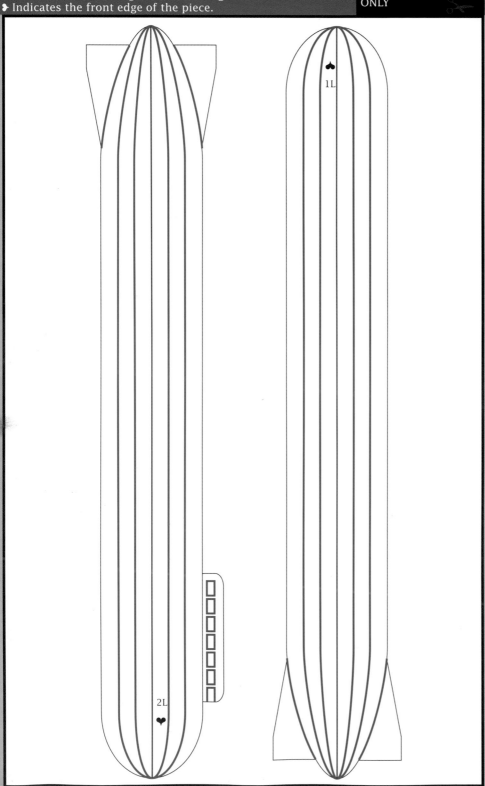

Count Ferdinand von Zeppelin was a big thinker. From the outset he conceived of enormous airships – great flying cigars. His first airship measured some 400 feet (120 m) in length. From there they only got bigger, the biggest to measure an incredible 803 feet (245 m). To support such a length of flexible material Zeppelin conceived of an internal metal framework, something like an enormous bridgework, to replace the external rope shrouds. Germany had recently seen the invention of the first internal combustion engine and Zeppelin fitted this to his monsters.

Early flight tests did not go well and it took him a long time to convince others that his large ships were airworthy. In the meantime, having spent all of his personal wealth on his dream, Zeppelin became broke. Surprisingly money poured in as people supported the Count, who had become a national hero. Zeppelin established the Zeppelin Foundation for the Promotion of Aerial Navigation, which allowed the company to go on to further develop and improve the rigid airship. Zeppelins became famous as the first airliners, circling the globe long before airplanes were able to do so.

Although these giant airships provided first-class service to rival that of the great ocean liners, because of their enormous size, airships were plagued with problems – mechanical

ZEPPELIN PIECES

- Cut on lines shown in black.
- Score lines in red.
- Use the blue lines as guides for adding details to the aircraft.
- ❥ Indicates the front edge of the piece.

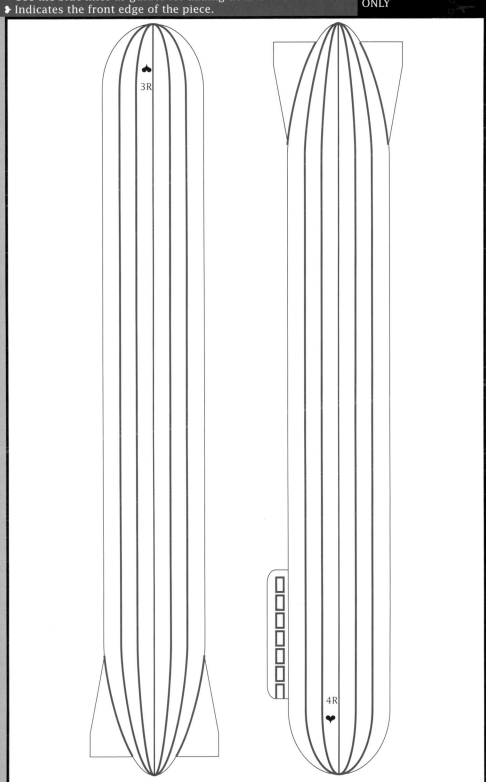

troubles, the effects of wind and weather, and not least, the danger of fire imposed by the large volume of flammable hydrogen gas. Although non-flammable helium gas had been discovered and was being used, it was in short supply and hydrogen was more often relied upon. Consequently many airships ended their days in flames.

Despite the dangers, Germany continued with airship service when others had already given up and in 1936 Zeppelin launched the LZ129 Hindenburg. It was luxurious and fast, traveling between Germany and the United States of America in under 50 hours. It was the pride of Germany. Safety was primary. Walkways were rubber coated to prevent sparks, no one was allowed to bring on board matches or lighters, and a special fireproof smoking lounge was provided.

Then in May of 1937, after a successful flight from Frankfurt to New Jersey where it docked, the mighty Hindenburg suddenly, inexplicably, caught fire, the flames quickly engulfing the entire ship. Incredibly only 35 of the 97 people on board were killed in the conflagration. This accident caused the public to lose confidence in airships and thus all further development of lighter-than-air commercial transportation ended.

1

Photocopy the layout pages
of pieces for this model.
Then cut out and prepare
the parts for assembly.
(See the general instructions
beginning on p 4.)

2

Bend pieces 1L through 4R
along center lines, as
shown.

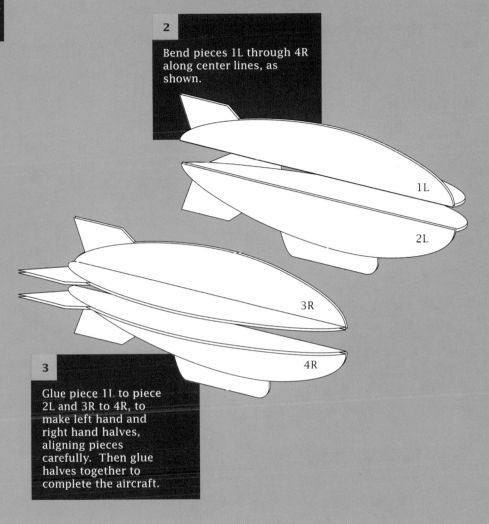

1L

2L

3R

4R

3

Glue piece 1L to piece
2L and 3R to 4R, to
make left hand and
right hand halves,
aligning pieces
carefully. Then glue
halves together to
complete the aircraft.

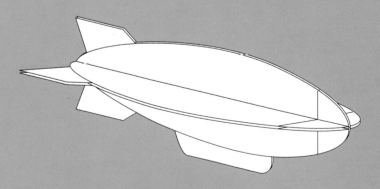

the finished
aircraft

THE PIECES

- Cut on lines shown in black.
- Score lines in red.
- Use the blue lines as guides for adding details to the aircraft.
- Indicates the front edge of the piece.

NOTE
CUT OUT PHOTOCOPY ONLY

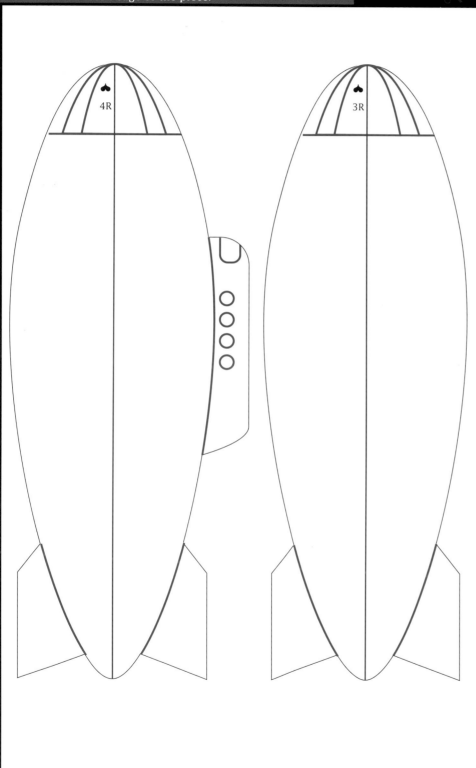

In the United States the Goodyear Tire and Rubber Company built airships, beginning in 1921 with the C7, which was used for coastal patrol by the Navy. From the outset American airships were filled with non-flammable helium gas, which was more expensive than hydrogen, but made airships safer from fire.

The Goodyear ships were at first non-rigid and were nick-named "blimps" from the fact that they were of B class and limp construction. Although rigid ships were built by this company, who even went into partnership with Zeppelin in 1928, Goodyear became better known for its blimps. Until 1935 a variety of rigid airships served in naval patrol. Thereafter patrol relied entirely on blimps. The American Navy used blimps for airborne early warning until 1962, when the last two Goodyear ZPG 3-W models were retired.

GOODYEAR PIECES

- Cut on lines shown in black.
- Score lines in red.
- Use the blue lines as guides for adding details to the aircraft.
- ❯ Indicates the front edge of the piece.

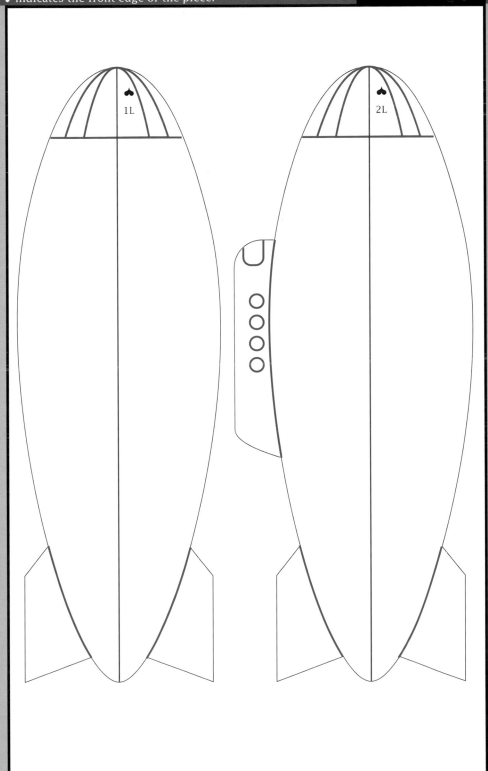

More recently Goodyear blimps have taken on a different role. They have been scaled down in size and fitted with tiltable ducted fan engines, making them more maneuverable and less prone to weather hazards. Now they have all the high-tech navigational aids found on airplanes. Incredibly, today these ships are seen frequently by large numbers of people. Their most common use is for overhead observation and advertising at large-scale public events such as fairs and games, and for short-range sightseeing trips.

Is there a broader future use for blimps? Because of their greatly improved reliability and maneuverablity, they are again being considered for their original role as patrol ships, as well as for "sky cranes" in such operations as logging in difficult-to-reach places where helicopters are also used.

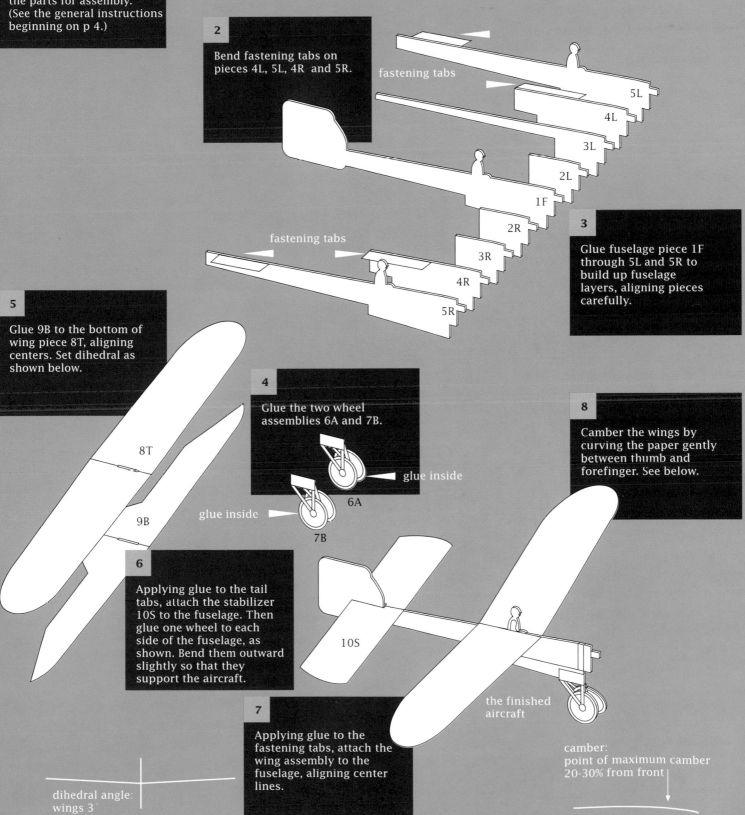

1

Photocopy the layout pages of pieces for this model. Then cut out and prepare the parts for assembly. (See the general instructions beginning on p 4.)

2

Bend fastening tabs on pieces 4L, 5L, 4R and 5R.

fastening tabs

5L

4L

3L

2L

1F

2R

fastening tabs

3R

4R

5R

3

Glue fuselage piece 1F through 5L and 5R to build up fuselage layers, aligning pieces carefully.

5

Glue 9B to the bottom of wing piece 8T, aligning centers. Set dihedral as shown below.

8T

9B

4

Glue the two wheel assemblies 6A and 7B.

glue inside

6A

glue inside

7B

8

Camber the wings by curving the paper gently between thumb and forefinger. See below.

6

Applying glue to the tail tabs, attach the stabilizer 10S to the fuselage. Then glue one wheel to each side of the fuselage, as shown. Bend them outward slightly so that they support the aircraft.

10S

the finished aircraft

7

Applying glue to the fastening tabs, attach the wing assembly to the fuselage, aligning center lines.

dihedral angle: wings 3°

camber:
point of maximum camber 20-30% from front

- Cut on lines shown in black.
- Score lines in red.
- Use the blue lines as guides for adding details to the aircraft.
- Indicates the front edge of the piece.

CUT OUT PHOTOCOPY ONLY

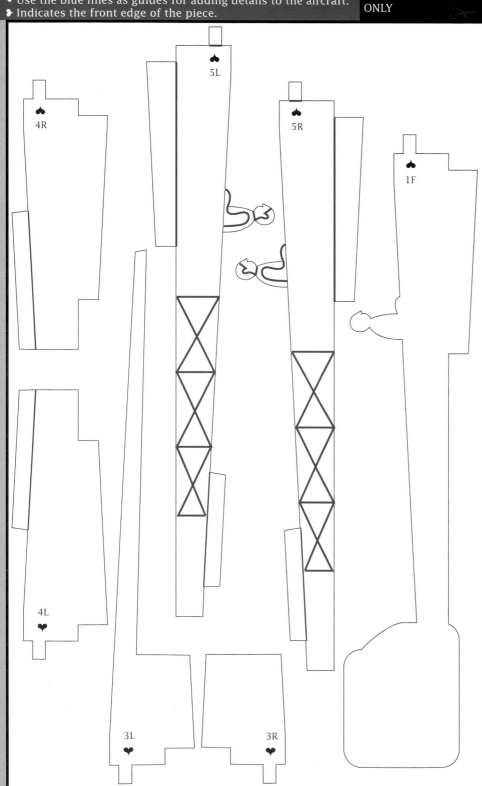

In 1903 successful sustained powered flight was achieved by Orville and Wilbur Wright, which spawned a flurry of invention and daring around the world. The Wright airplanes were biplanes modeled on the box kite of the day, a rigid cross-braced stucture having two pairs of wings. But Louis Bleriot of France had different ideas for aircraft. His designs were flimsy monoplanes that expressed his flambouyant and daring personality.

Louis Bleriot was not only a dreamer but also an achiever. As did other individuals in his day, he designed, built, and flew his own airplanes. This resulted in many crashes but knowledge was gained about flight through trial and error – a dangerous proposition in aviation. These aircraft designs were based on intuition more than on scientific knowledge. Incredibly, in Bleriot's career, he survived all but the last of thirty-three crashes.

BLERIOT PIECES

- Cut on lines shown in black.
- Score lines in red.
- Use the blue lines as guides for adding details to the aircraft.
- Indicates the front edge of the piece.

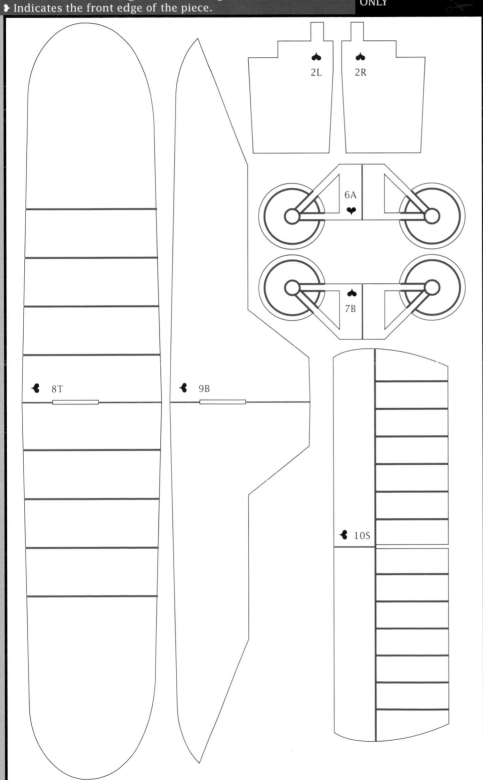

Bleriot's monoplane design was ahead of its time. Many variations of the design were built by Bleriot and others. However, many of them broke up in flight because the stresses on the airframes were greater than the strength that could be built into the mono structures using the knowledge they had. Despite this, 800 Bleriot XI monoplanes were built. After this monoplanes mostly disappeared from the skies until the 1930s when stronger airframes could be built.

The greatest fame of the Bleriot monoplane came in 1909 when Bleriot changed the world by flying across the English Channel from Calais to Dover. Newspapers of the day prophetically proclaimed that England was no longer an island, because the protection afforded Great Britain by the sea had been breached.

Spirit of
St.Louis

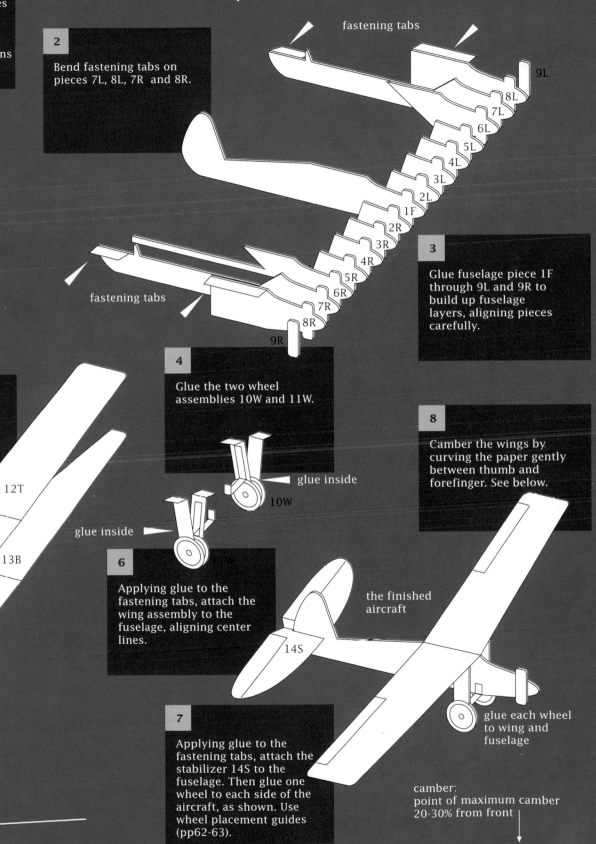

1

Photocopy the layout pages of pieces for this model. Then cut out and prepare the parts for assembly. (See the general instructions beginning on p 4.)

2

Bend fastening tabs on pieces 7L, 8L, 7R and 8R.

fastening tabs

9L
8L
7L
6L
5L
4L
3L
2L
1F
2R
3R
4R
5R
6R
7R
8R
9R

fastening tabs

3

Glue fuselage piece 1F through 9L and 9R to build up fuselage layers, aligning pieces carefully.

5

Glue 13B to the bottom of wing piece 12T, aligning centers. Set dihedral as shown below.

12T

13B

4

Glue the two wheel assemblies 10W and 11W.

glue inside

10W

glue inside

11W

8

Camber the wings by curving the paper gently between thumb and forefinger. See below.

6

Applying glue to the fastening tabs, attach the wing assembly to the fuselage, aligning center lines.

the finished aircraft

14S

glue each wheel to wing and fuselage

7

Applying glue to the fastening tabs, attach the stabilizer 14S to the fuselage. Then glue one wheel to each side of the aircraft, as shown. Use wheel placement guides (pp62-63).

dihedral angle: wings 3°

camber: point of maximum camber 20-30% from front

THE PIECES

lindbergh

- Cut on lines shown in black.
- Score lines in red.
- Use the blue lines as guides for adding details to the aircraft.
➤ Indicates the front edge of the piece.

CUT OUT PHOTOCOPY ONLY

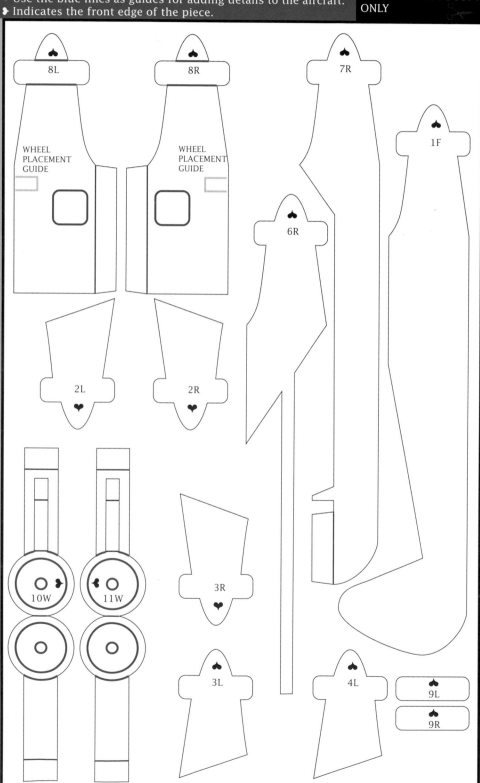

The pioneers of aviation knew that their machines were extremely fragile, under-powered, and of limited use. To encourage the development of airplanes, prizes were offered by wealthy corporations for various aerial feats. This hastened their improvement, but after the war of 1914-18 aviation fell into a slump and prizes and sponsorships were continued as the main incentive to support the industry. In 1913 the Daily Mail newspaper of London announced a £10,000 prize for non-stop flight across the Atlantic ocean. This offer still stood after the war ended, and was achieved only in 1919 when John Alcock and Arthur Brown flew a Vickers Vimy from Newfoundland to Ireland in 16 hours 27 minutes. Some 92 successful trans-Atlantic flights were made, but all were done with multiple crews flying multiengined machines. To encourage a solo crossing a $25,000 prize was offered.

LINDBERGH PIECES

- Cut on lines shown in black.
- Score lines in red.
- Use the blue lines as guides for adding details to the aircraft.
- ◗ Indicates the front edge of the piece.

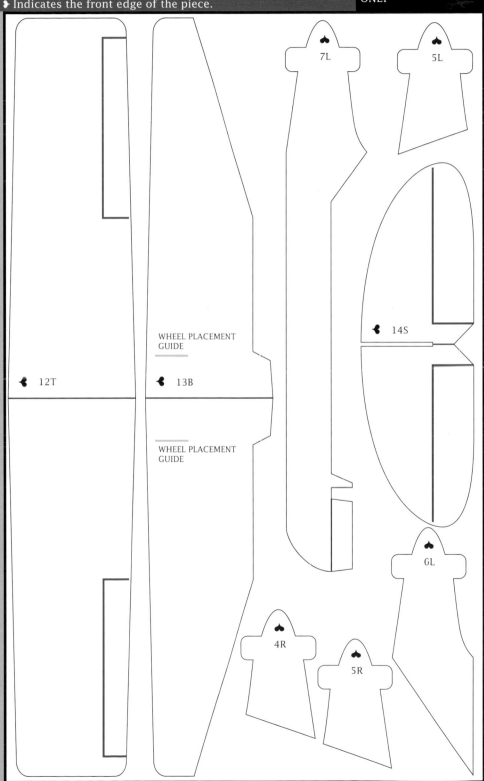

Charles Lindbergh, an American Army Air Service and US Mail Service pilot, dreamed of winning this prize. He looked to Ryan Airlines Inc. to provide an airplane suited to the job. Their model B1 was an all-metal monoplane. This strong airframe was fitted with a Wright Whirlwind air-cooled radial engine, already proven to be reliable. In addition to this, a large fuel tank was installed. Incredibly, this completely blocked all forward vision. With barely enough power to lift the enormous load of fuel, the Spirit of St Louis made the solo flight in May of 1927, taking 33 hours 30 minutes to fly from New York to Paris. This was an incredible test for man and machine involving endurance, piloting skill, and navigation. Lindbergh was a worldwide hero, the Wright engine became a world standard, all-metal monoplanes replaced wood and fabric biplanes, and aviation was given a kick-start as thousands of individuals turned their attention to flight.

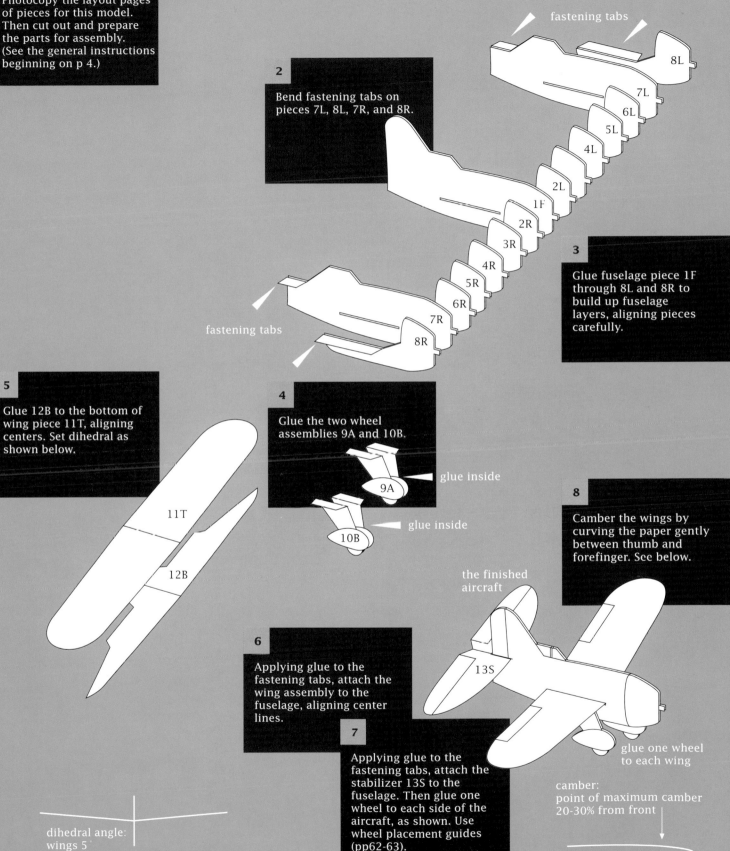

1

Photocopy the layout pages of pieces for this model. Then cut out and prepare the parts for assembly. (See the general instructions beginning on p 4.)

2

Bend fastening tabs on pieces 7L, 8L, 7R, and 8R.

fastening tabs

8L
7L
6L
5L
4L
2L
1F
2R
3R
4R
5R
6R
7R
8R

fastening tabs

3

Glue fuselage piece 1F through 8L and 8R to build up fuselage layers, aligning pieces carefully.

5

Glue 12B to the bottom of wing piece 11T, aligning centers. Set dihedral as shown below.

11T
12B

4

Glue the two wheel assemblies 9A and 10B.

9A

glue inside

10B

glue inside

8

Camber the wings by curving the paper gently between thumb and forefinger. See below.

the finished aircraft

13S

6

Applying glue to the fastening tabs, attach the wing assembly to the fuselage, aligning center lines.

7

Applying glue to the fastening tabs, attach the stabilizer 13S to the fuselage. Then glue one wheel to each side of the aircraft, as shown. Use wheel placement guides (pp62-63).

glue one wheel to each wing

camber: point of maximum camber 20-30% from front

dihedral angle: wings 5°

THE PIECES

- Cut on lines shown in black.
- Score lines in red.
- Use the blue lines as guides for adding details to the aircraft.
- ❥ Indicates the front edge of the piece.

CUT OUT PHOTOCOPY ONLY

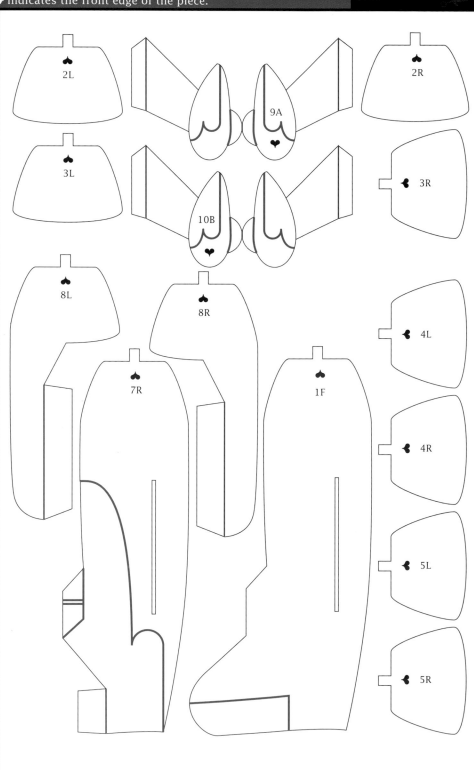

2L

3L

9A

10B

8L

8R

7R

1F

2R

3R

4L

4R

5L

5R

The success of Lindbergh's flight spawned a variety of public aerial events worldwide. The public could not get enough of the excitement that flight provided. Among the events were two famous annual races in the United States. The Thompson Trophy Race was a closed-circuit round-the-pylon race and the Bendix Trophy Race was a long-distance cross-country race. Such events kept aviation in the forefront of public attention at a time when the commercial use of airplanes was not yet widely established.

In 1932 Granville Bros. Aircraft was formed by members of the Granville family and a few hired hands. Their goal was to build an airplane that would go fast. The elder brother Zantford, known as "Granny," was an intuitive engineer. He conceived of an airframe that could fly both pylon and long-distance races utilizing a different engine for each. This was the Gee Bee Model R.

GEE BEE PIECES

- Cut on lines shown in black.
- Score lines in red.
- Use the blue lines as guides for adding details to the aircraft.
- Indicates the front edge of the piece.

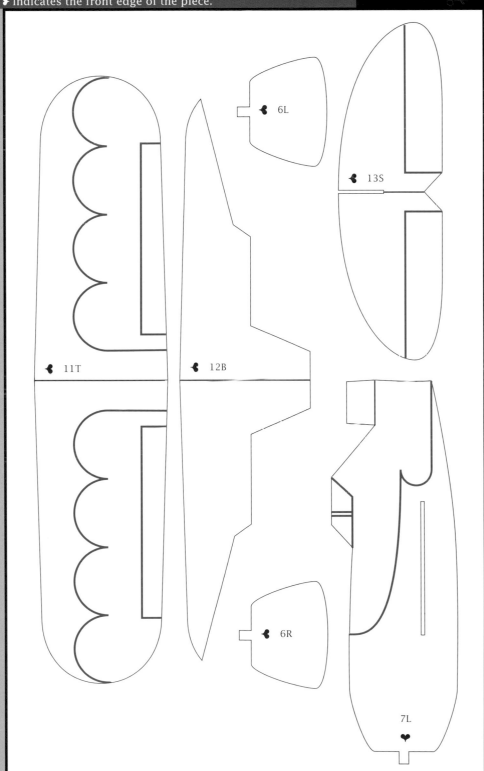

The R model was, in fact, mostly engine. The Granvilles wind tunnel tested the smallest possible airframe for the largest possible engine. This small airplane looks something like a barrel with stubby wings.

In 1932 this plane, powered by an 800 hp Pratt and Whitney Wasp engine, won the Thompson trophy at a speed of 252 mph. The Gee Bee Model R has become a plane of legend, not for what it achieved, but for an impression left in the public mind that it was a dangerous beast. Thousands witnessed not only the successful racing of this incredible machine but also two spectacular crashes, one of which was forever captured on film.

Although somewhat unstable, the airplane was a great machine and successful racer. Today a replica has been built by Delmar Benjamin and is flown at many airshows to the delight of large crowds.

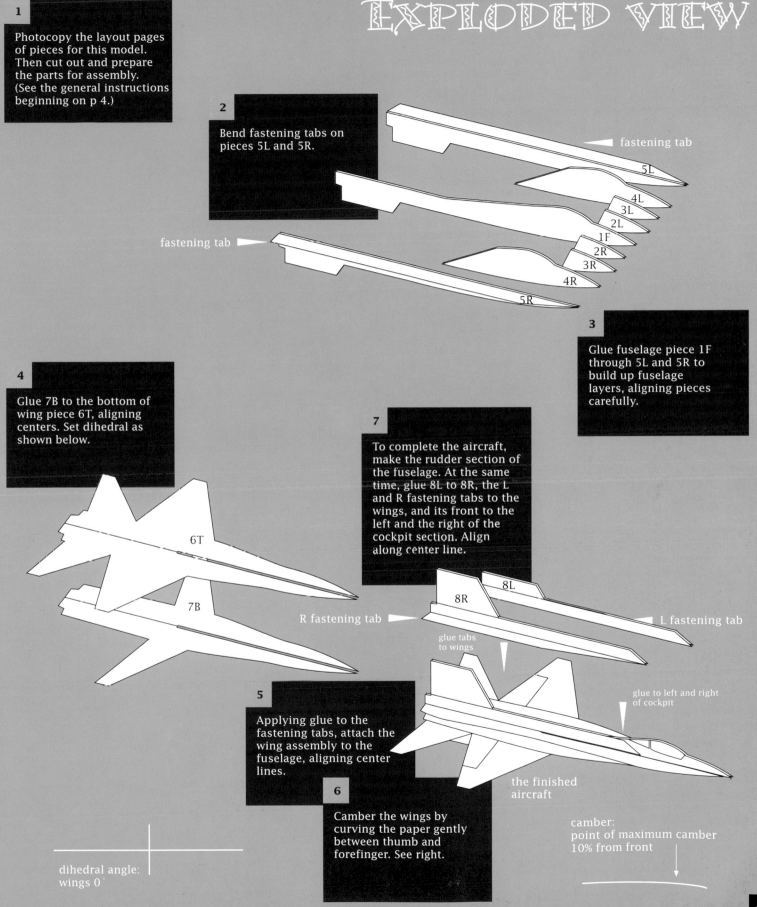

1
Photocopy the layout pages of pieces for this model. Then cut out and prepare the parts for assembly. (See the general instructions beginning on p 4.)

2
Bend fastening tabs on pieces 5L and 5R.

fastening tab

5L
4L
3L
2L
1F
2R
3R
4R
5R

fastening tab

3
Glue fuselage piece 1F through 5L and 5R to build up fuselage layers, aligning pieces carefully.

4
Glue 7B to the bottom of wing piece 6T, aligning centers. Set dihedral as shown below.

6T
7B

7
To complete the aircraft, make the rudder section of the fuselage. At the same time, glue 8L to 8R, the L and R fastening tabs to the wings, and its front to the left and the right of the cockpit section. Align along center line.

8L
8R

R fastening tab

L fastening tab

glue tabs to wings

glue to left and right of cockpit

the finished aircraft

5
Applying glue to the fastening tabs, attach the wing assembly to the fuselage, aligning center lines.

6
Camber the wings by curving the paper gently between thumb and forefinger. See right.

dihedral angle: wings 0°

camber: point of maximum camber 10% from front

- Cut on lines shown in black.
- Score lines in red.
- Use the blue lines as guides for adding details to the aircraft.
- ❧ Indicates the front edge of the piece.

NOTE
CUT OUT PHOTOCOPY
ONLY

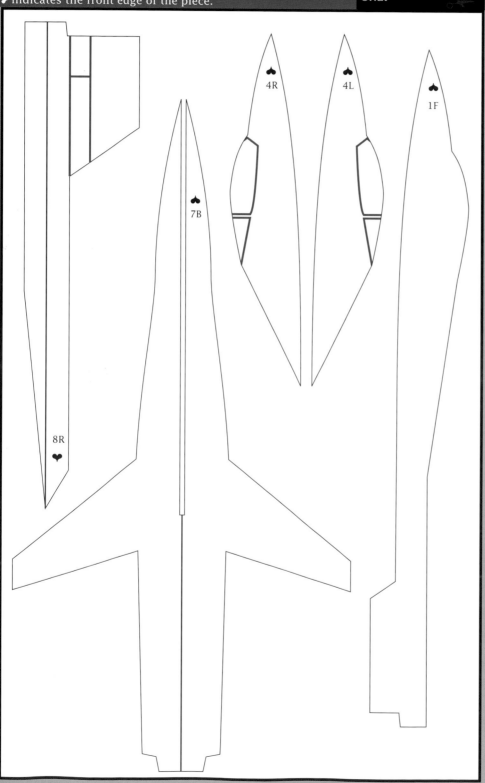

It was thought at one time that the best way to leave the earth's atmosphere would be to fly an airplane high enough and fast enough to go into low earth orbit. Consequently a call for an experimental airplane that could fly to the edge of the atmosphere came from the National Advisory Committee for Aeronautics (now National Aeronautics and Space Administration) as early as 1950, three years after the X-1 had first broken the sound barrier, which is a speed of about 740 mph called Mach 1. A hypersonic study team was brought together, who by 1954, had developed the primary concept for such an aircraft.

Hypersonic meant speeds of between Mach 5 and 7. Three things were evident: that the aircraft be powered by rocket engine, since no jets were thought to be powerful enough for the task; that new materials were needed to withstand the stresses; and that it be "piggy-back" launched to avoid the problems of ground takeoff (mainly the need for a large quantity of fuel).

X-15 PIECES

- Cut on lines shown in black.
- Score lines in red.
- Use the blue lines as guides for adding details to the aircraft.
- ❯ Indicates the front edge of the piece.

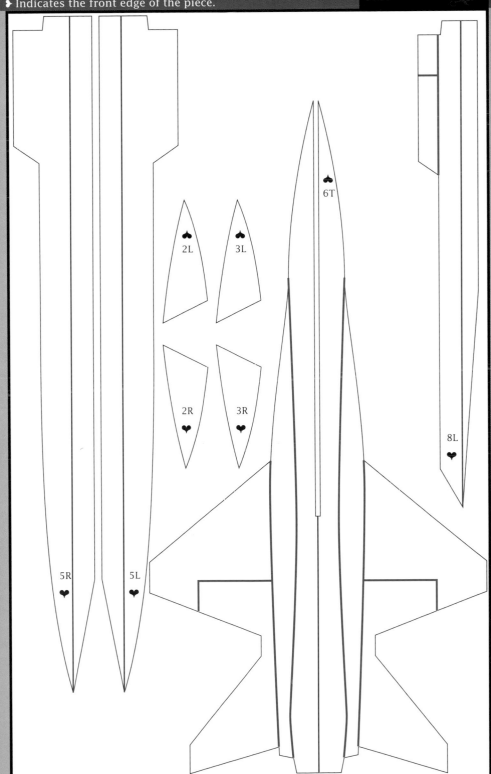

The X-15 was the result, built by the North American Company, using super-alloys for strength and special coatings made from resins, catalyst, and glass bead powder to protect it from the extreme heat caused by air friction. It was 50 feet long with a 22 foot wingspan and 11 foot tail. It was powered by one throttleable YLR-99 rocket engine that burned a mixture of anhydrous ammonia and liquid oxygen with a 2 minute burn time and 57,000 pounds of thrust. In addition to this it had small reaction thrusters to steer the plane at subspace altitudes where there was not enough air for the wings and tail to be operational.

Although the idea of flying into space with an airplane was dropped in exchange for blasting off in the mid-60s, the X-15 provided much useful information about transatmospheric flight. It achieved Mach 6.7 at 354,200 feet (106,260 m). The pilots qualified for astronaut's wings before there were any orbital flights.

1

Photocopy the layout pages of pieces for this model. Then cut out and prepare the parts for assembly. (See the general instructions beginning on p 4.)

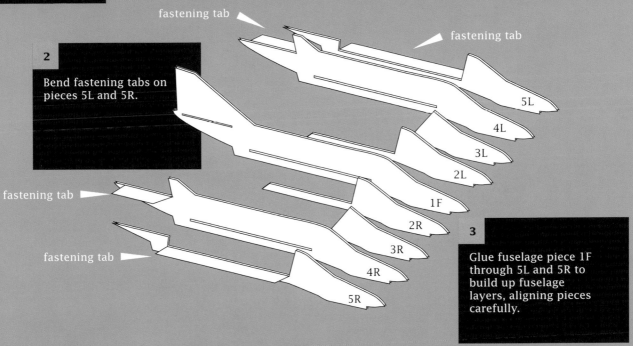

fastening tab

fastening tab

2

Bend fastening tabs on pieces 5L and 5R.

5L

4L

3L

2L

1F

2R

3R

4R

5R

fastening tab

fastening tab

3

Glue fuselage piece 1F through 5L and 5R to build up fuselage layers, aligning pieces carefully.

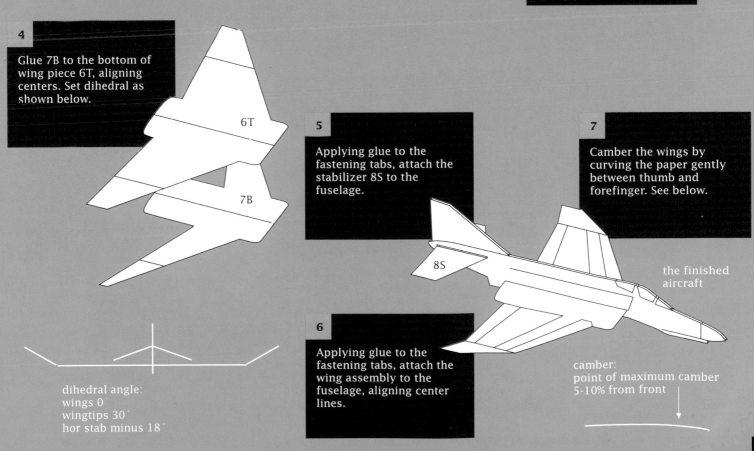

4

Glue 7B to the bottom of wing piece 6T, aligning centers. Set dihedral as shown below.

6T

7B

5

Applying glue to the fastening tabs, attach the stabilizer 8S to the fuselage.

7

Camber the wings by curving the paper gently between thumb and forefinger. See below.

8S

the finished aircraft

6

Applying glue to the fastening tabs, attach the wing assembly to the fuselage, aligning center lines.

dihedral angle:
wings 0°
wingtips 30°
hor stab minus 18°

camber:
point of maximum camber 5-10% from front

THE PIECES

- Cut on lines shown in black.
- Score lines in red.
- Use the blue lines as guides for adding details to the aircraft.
- Indicates the front edge of the piece.

CUT OUT PHOTOCOPY
ONLY

This airplane, built by McDonnell Douglas, is one of the most numerous fighters to be built after the Second World War. It was in production from 1959 through 1979, with more than 5000 being built in the United States and Japan. Incredibly it remains in service with at least ten countries and will continue service well into the 21st century, giving it the longest service life of any fighter.

It was assumed that fighter planes would no longer need to be armed with guns after the advent of supersonic flight with jet propulsion and air-to-air rockets. The Phantom was therefore the first to be built without gun armament. It was soon discovered, however, that this was a false assumption, and provisions were made to add a gun pod underneath.

In fact, this airplane, designed to be either land or carrier based, boasts many firsts, one of which

F-4 PIECES

- Cut on lines shown in black.
- Score lines in red.
- Use the blue lines as guides for adding details to the aircraft.
- ❥ Indicates the front edge of the piece.

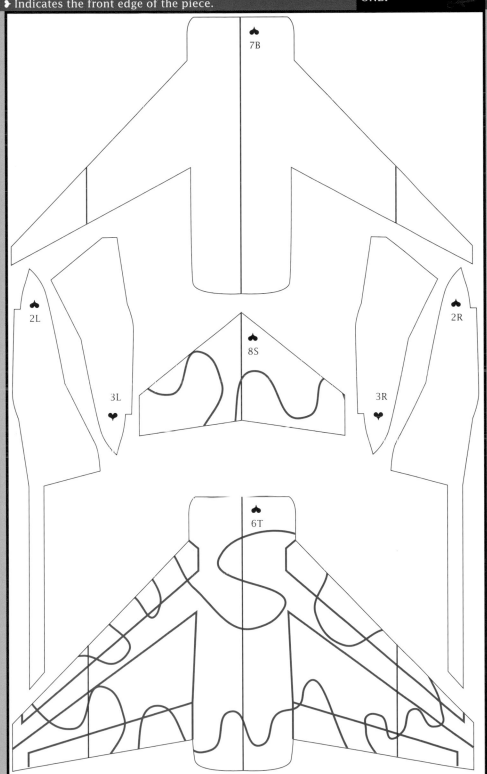

was the ability to hang a great variety of armaments from the airframe hardpoints. This made it into a very versatile machine, that is one of the keys to its success. It was also the first fighter to utilize electronics to manage engine systems to optimize power output, as well as to search for, identify, and destroy targets that were beyond visual range, without support from ground control. This twin-engine afterburning turbojet flies at Mach 2 and has a service altitude of 40,000 feet.

Over the years some 30 variants of the Phantom have been made. In the 1960s this airplane was the pride of the aeronautical establishment and demonstrated the height of aeronautical achievement. As a consequence it was flown at air shows by the display teams of the US Navy Blue Angels and the US Air Force Thunderbirds simultaneously.

18 LOCKHEED SR-71 blackbird

1
Photocopy the layout pages of pieces for this model. Then cut out and prepare the parts for assembly. (See the general instructions beginning on p 4.)

2
Bend fastening tabs on pieces 4L and 4R. Also on stiffening pieces 5L and 5R and vertical stabilizer/ engine pieces 6L, 6R, 7L, and 7R.

fastening tab

4L

3L

2L

1F

2R

3R

4R

fastening tab

3
Glue fuselage piece 1F through 4L and 4R to build up fuselage layers, aligning pieces carefully.

4
Glue 9B to the bottom of wing piece 8T, aligning centers. Set dihedral as shown below.

5
Glue piece 7L to 6L and 7R to 6R to make the vertical stabilizer/engine assemblies. Applying glue to tabs, attach them to the wings, aligning carefully. Set angle as shown below.

7
Applying glue to pieces 5L and 5R, attach them to the left and right hand sides of the fuselage as stiffeners so that the tabs attach to the upper wing surfaces.

6L

7L

fastening tab

fastening tab

fastening tab

6R

fastening tab

7R

8T

9B

L fastening tab

R fastening tab

5R

5L

8
Camber the wings by curving the paper gently between thumb and forefinger. See below.

the finished aircraft

6
Applying glue to the fastening tabs, attach the wing assembly to the fuselage, aligning center lines.

dihedral angle:
wings 0˚
vert stab 20˚

camber:
point of maximum camber 5-10% from front

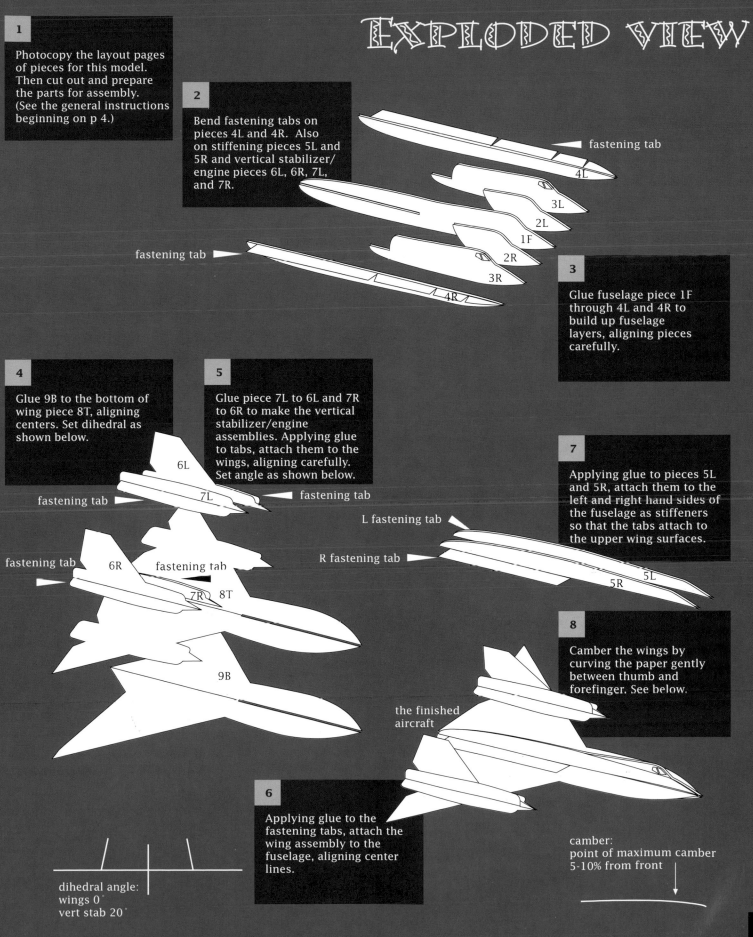

THE PIECES

- Cut on lines shown in black.
- Score lines in red.
- Use the blue lines as guides for adding details to the aircraft.
- Indicates the front edge of the piece.

CUT OUT PHOTOCOPY ONLY

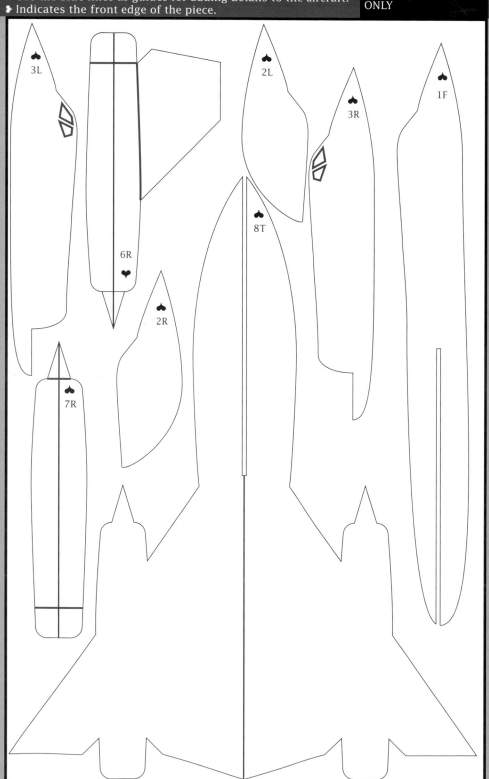

The SR-71 was designed for one purpose only: to take pictures while flying high and fast. In fact, it flew so high and fast that no enemy armaments of any kind could touch it. It was a global strategic reconnaissance spy plane.

The incredible pictures taken by this airplane are so sharp that they reveal objects as small as a golfball from an altitude of 80,000 feet (24,000 m). In each hour of flight more than 100,000 square miles (260,000 sq km) of the earth's surface are photographed.

When this airplane was being developed in the late 1950s-early 60s, no technology existed to accomplish the task of building components that could withstand the stresses of such flight. It was under the leadership of Kelly Johnson, legendary designer with Lockheed, that the work was accomplished. The airframe is built primarily of very strong and lightweight titanium as well as compos-

SR-71 PIECES

- Cut on lines shown in black.
- Score lines in red.
- Use the blue lines as guides for adding details to the aircraft.
- ❧ Indicates the front edge of the piece.

CUT OUT PHOTOCOPY ONLY

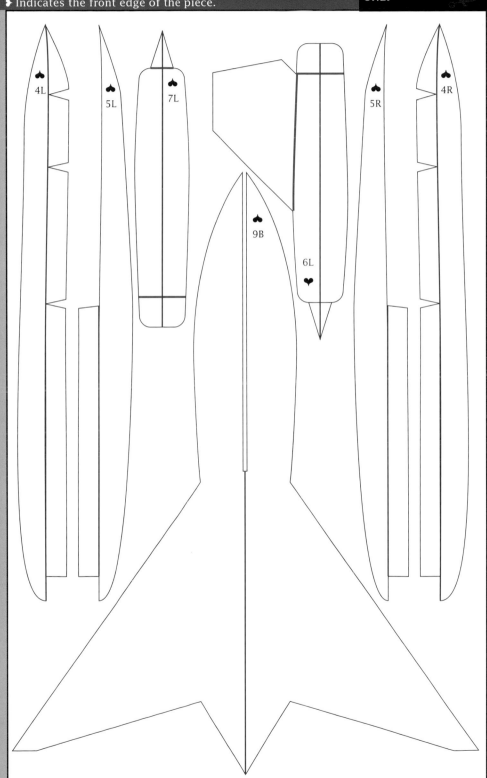

ite plastics. Because of the extreme temperature changes that the aircraft would be subjected to, special expansion joints were needed to allow for changes in the size of components. In flight the skin of the plane heats to 800 degrees F (427˚ C) from air friction and the entire airframe increases in length by six inches (15 cm).

The SR-71 is powered by two Pratt and Whitney axial-flow turbojets with special afterburners, which, at a maximum cruise speed of over Mach 3, produce most of the power. This incredible plane is the fastest and highest flying air breathing machine, setting an absolute speed record of 2,194 mph at a record-setting altitude of 85,068 feet (25,520 m). It carries enough fuel to maintain this speed for one hour and can be refuelled in flight (at a slower speed and lower altitude, of course). While no longer in active service, two are used for flight research by NASA.

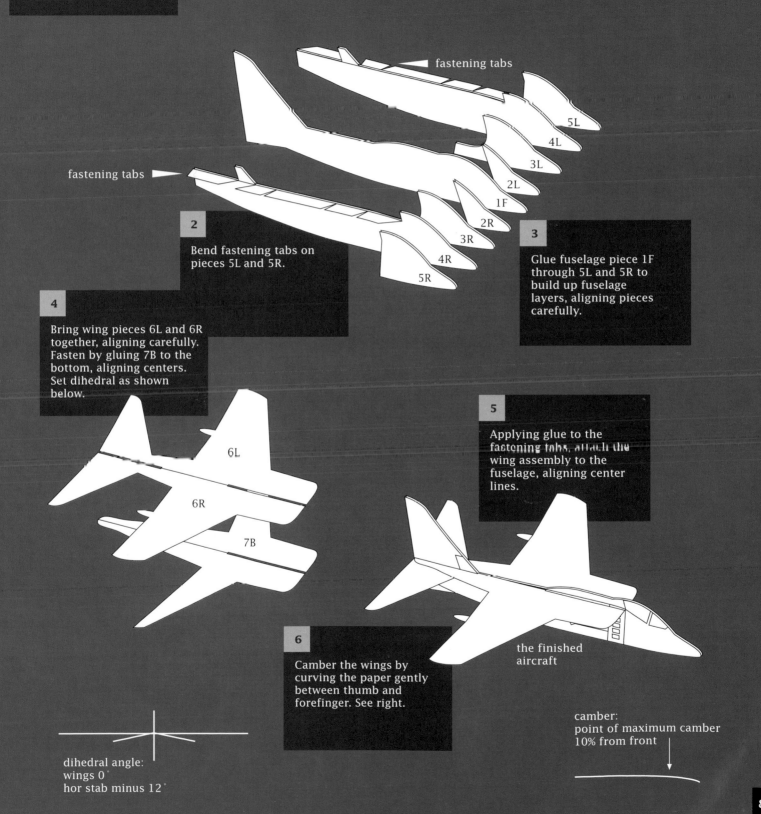

1

Photocopy the layout pages of pieces for this model. Then cut out and prepare the parts for assembly. (See the general instructions beginning on p 4.)

fastening tabs

fastening tabs

5L
4L
3L
2L
1F
2R
3R
4R
5R

2

Bend fastening tabs on pieces 5L and 5R.

3

Glue fuselage piece 1F through 5L and 5R to build up fuselage layers, aligning pieces carefully.

4

Bring wing pieces 6L and 6R together, aligning carefully. Fasten by gluing 7B to the bottom, aligning centers. Set dihedral as shown below.

6L
6R
7B

5

Applying glue to the fastening tabs, attach the wing assembly to the fuselage, aligning center lines.

6

Camber the wings by curving the paper gently between thumb and forefinger. See right.

the finished aircraft

dihedral angle:
wings 0°
hor stab minus 12°

camber:
point of maximum camber
10% from front

- Cut on lines shown in black.
- Score lines in red.
- Use the blue lines as guides for adding details to the aircraft.
- ❯ Indicates the front edge of the piece.

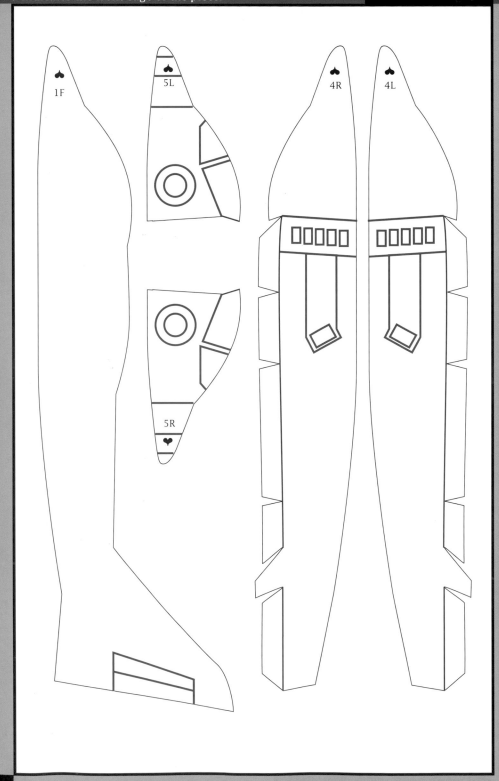

Air forces have long realized that for military purposes the need for a runway is a liability. Runways in battle are easy targets and hard to maintain. During the 1950s a variety of experimental aircraft capable of taking off vertically without the need of a runway was built. The problem was not the vertical takeoff so much as the transition to horizontal flight. In 1960 the British company Hawker Siddeley was the first to build an experimental airplane that could successfully take off vertically, hover, and transition to horizontal flight and then back to vertical landing. But it was not until 1969 that the plane was suitably safe to be made operational as a fighter. Even then, it was not an easy aircraft to pilot.

A pair of vectoring (rotatable) jet nozzles on each side of the fuselage direct the engine thrust vertically or horizontally to achieve the desired direction of flight. In addition to these, small puffer nozzles in the wingtips and tail

HARRIER PIECES

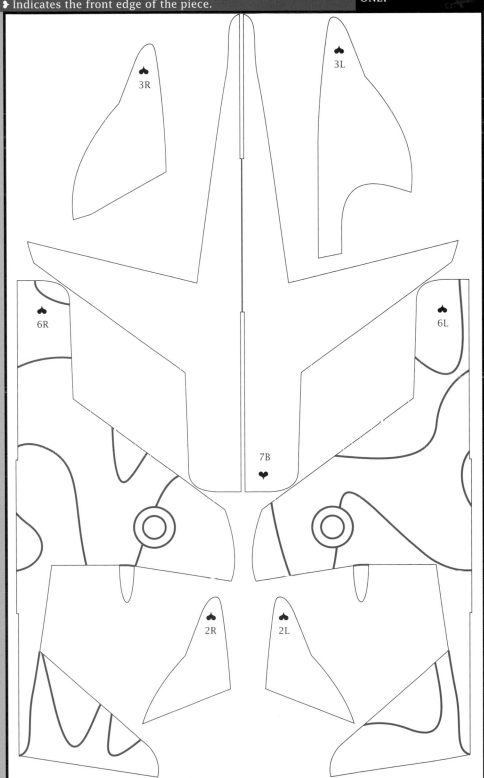

help maintain stability. When the nozzles are directed straight back the plane performs just like an ordinary jet. In 1975 McDonnell Douglas began to work with Hawker Siddeley in the development of an advanced version. The resulting plane has composite wings to produce greater lift, better cruise capabilities, more fuel carrying capacity, and has better all-around handling characteristics.

The biggest advantages of the Harrier are that it can operate close to the battle lines, be hidden easily from enemy view, and still take off at a moment's notice when needed. At sea, Harriers can operate from much smaller aircraft carriers, have simpler operations, and save substantial costs. Besides the UK and USA, this incredible machine is used by the Armed Services of several countries, and has proven to be a versatile multirole military aircraft that will remain in service for a long time into the future.

20 voyager

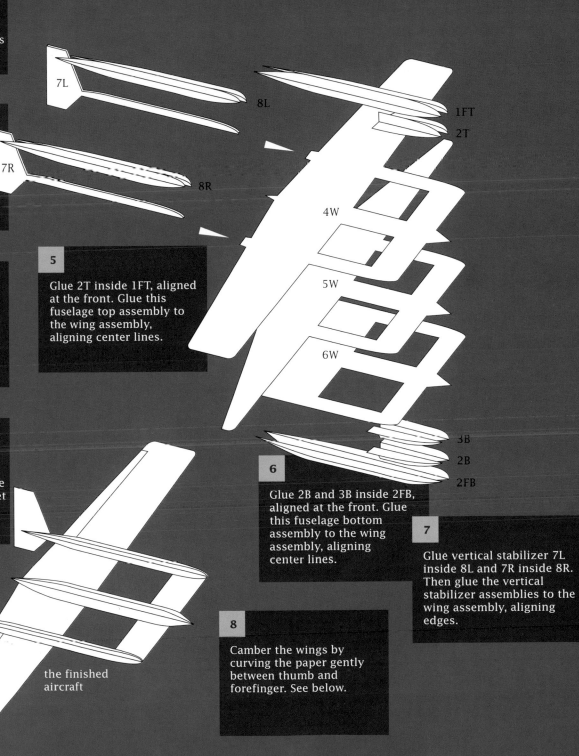

1

Photocopy the layout pages of pieces for this model. Then cut out and prepare the parts for assembly. (See the general instructions beginning on p 4.)

2

Bend pieces 1FT, 2T, 8L, and 8R, as shown.

(view from front)

3

Bend pieces 2FB, 2B, and 3B, as shown.

(view from front)

4

Glue 5W to the bottom of wing piece 4W, aligning centers. Then add 6W to the bottom of this assembly. Set dihedral as shown below.

5

Glue 2T inside 1FT, aligned at the front. Glue this fuselage top assembly to the wing assembly, aligning center lines.

6

Glue 2B and 3B inside 2FB, aligned at the front. Glue this fuselage bottom assembly to the wing assembly, aligning center lines.

7

Glue vertical stabilizer 7L inside 8L and 7R inside 8R. Then glue the vertical stabilizer assemblies to the wing assembly, aligning edges.

8

Camber the wings by curving the paper gently between thumb and forefinger. See below.

the finished aircraft

dihedral angle: wings 2°

camber: point of maximum camber 20-30% from front

THE PIECES

- Cut on lines shown in black.
- Score lines in red.
- Use the blue lines as guides for adding details to the aircraft.
- ⤐ Indicates the front edge of the piece.

CUT OUT PHOTOCOPY ONLY

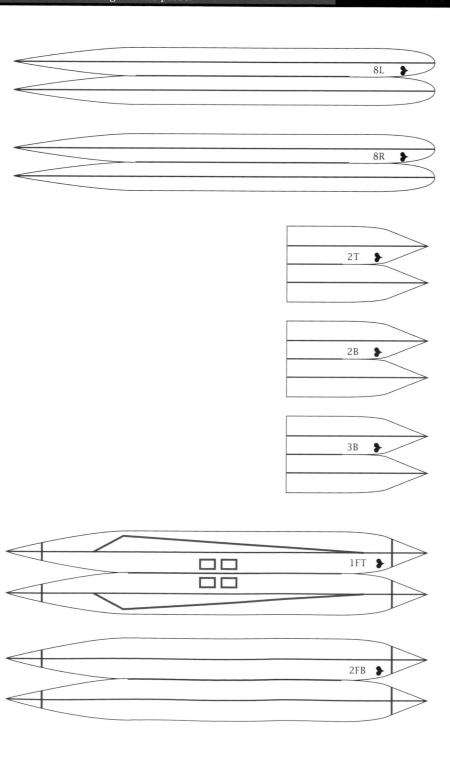

8L

8R

2T

2B

3B

1FT

2FB

Circumnavigating the earth began with ocean-going ships in the 15th century and took as long as 3 years. Since then ships have become faster but still require weeks for the voyage. The goal of airplanes, however, was to fly around the world in a much shorter time. The first such flight took place in 1924. The approximately 25,000 mile (40,000 km) journey was done in stages of short flights by two open cockpit biplanes, and took 175 days. This was bettered by a Graf Zeppelin airship in 1929, and was completed with only 3 refueling stops

VOYAGER PIECES

- Cut on lines shown in black.
- Score lines in red.
- Use the blue lines as guides for adding details to the aircraft.
- ❥ Indicates the front edge of the piece.

NOTE
CUT OUT PHOTOCOPY
ONLY

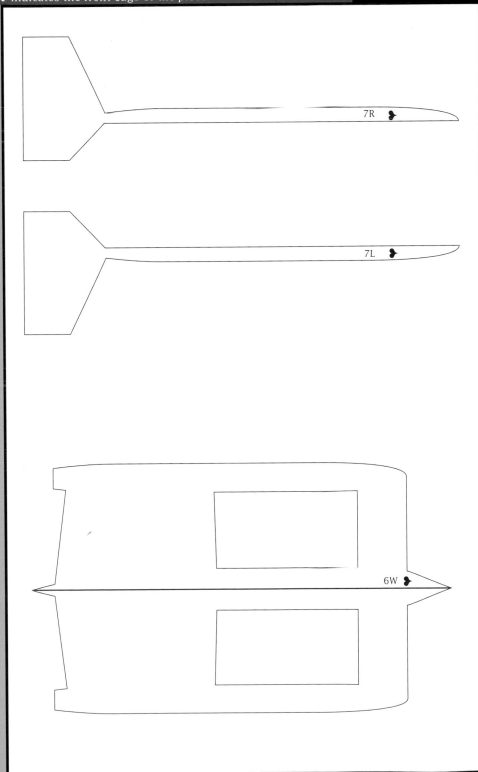

in 21 days. Encouraged by Charles Lindbergh's transatlantic flight, Wiley Post and navigator Harold Gatty, in 1931, flew the distance in a single-engined Lockheed Vega in just 8 days. Two years later Post, in the same aircraft, did it solo in 7 days. The first non-stop flight was done in 1949 by a B-52 bomber, but took multiple in-flight refuelings. The last aero-circumnavigational challenge was a non-stop non-refueled flight. The Voyager was built especially for this task.

VOYAGER PIECES

- Cut on lines shown in black.
- Score lines in red.
- Use the blue lines as guides for adding details to the aircraft.
- ❯ Indicates the front edge of the piece.

NOTE:
CUT OUT PHOTOCOPY ONLY

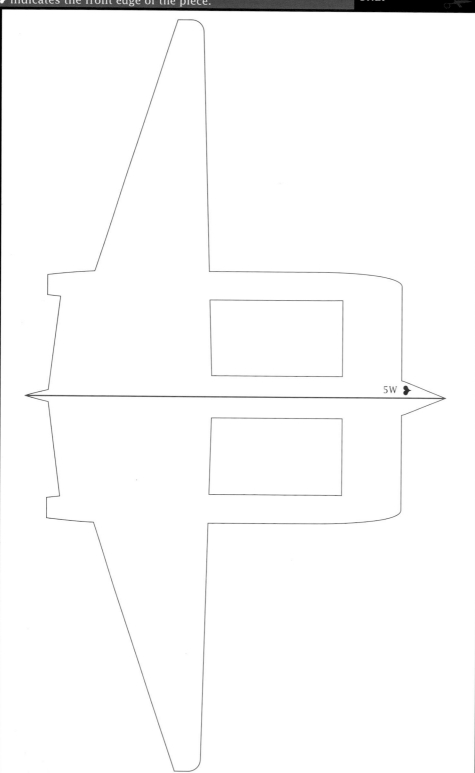

5W

The people who would pilot the Voyager, Dick Rutan and Jeana Yeager, were also involved in designing, building, and testing it, over a period of 6 years. A major design challenge for such an aircraft was to match the fuel consumption to the amount carried. And fuel consumption further depended on the efficiency of the airframe and the powerplant. In the end, the plane was mainly a flying fuel tank – tanks actually. It had a total of 17, and fuel had to be shifted from tank to tank during flight to retain balance. The canard

• Cut on lines shown in black.
• Score lines in red.
• Use the blue lines as guides for adding details to the aircraft.
➤ Indicates the front edge of the piece.

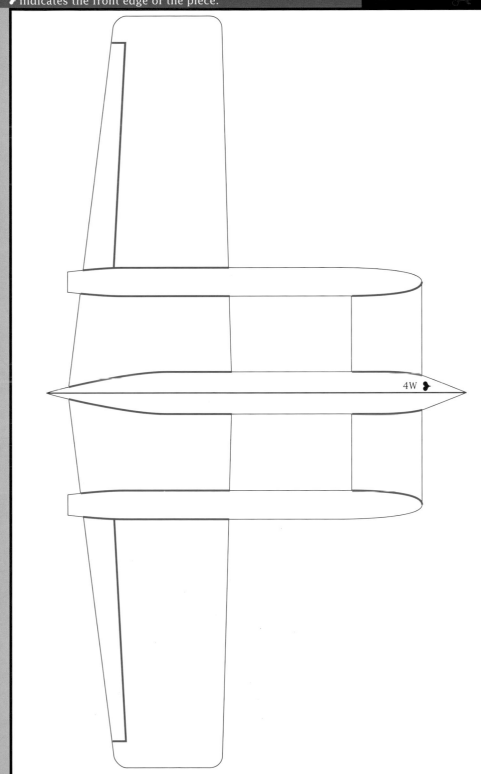

4W ➤

airframe was made of lightweight composite materials with long slender wings that were so flexible that, loaded with fuel, the wingtips rested on the ground and in flight flexed upward 5 feet (1.5 m). Propulsion came from two engines, one at each end of the fuselage, with the front one used only during critical times. The flight, completed just before Christmas 1986, took 9 days. Incredibly, of the 1300 gallons (5800 l) of fuel taken only 11 (49 l) remained at landing.

space shuttle

1

Photocopy the layout pages of pieces for this model. Then cut out and prepare the parts for assembly. (See the general instructions beginning on p 4.)

2

Bend fastening tabs on top fuselage pieces 4L and 4R and on bottom fuselage pieces 2BL and 2BR.

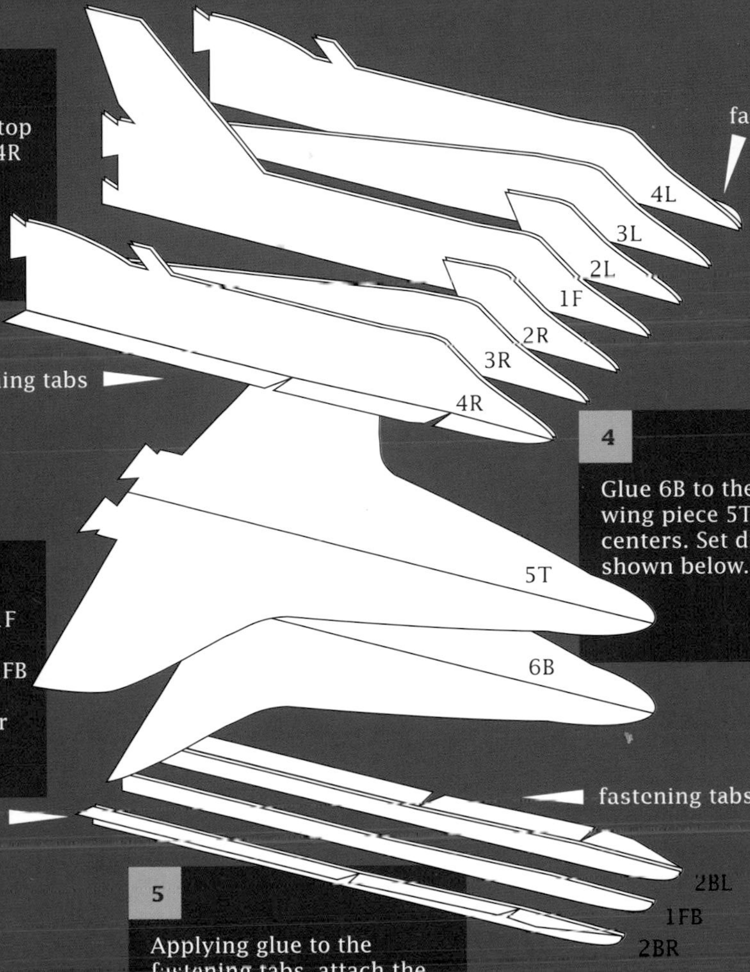

fastening tabs

4L

3L

2L

1F

2R

3R

4R

fastening tabs ▶

4

Glue 6B to the bottom of wing piece 5T, aligning centers. Set dihedral as shown below.

5T

6B

3

Glue top fuselage piece 1F through 4L and 4R and bottom fuselage pieces 1FB through 2BL and 2BR to build up upper and lower fuselage layers, aligning pieces carefully.

fastening tabs ▶

◀ fastening tabs

2BL

1FB

2BR

5

Applying glue to the fastening tabs, attach the upper fuselage assembly to the wing assembly, aligning center lines. Repeat with bottom fuselage assembly.

6

Camber the wings by curving the paper gently between thumb and forefinger. See below.

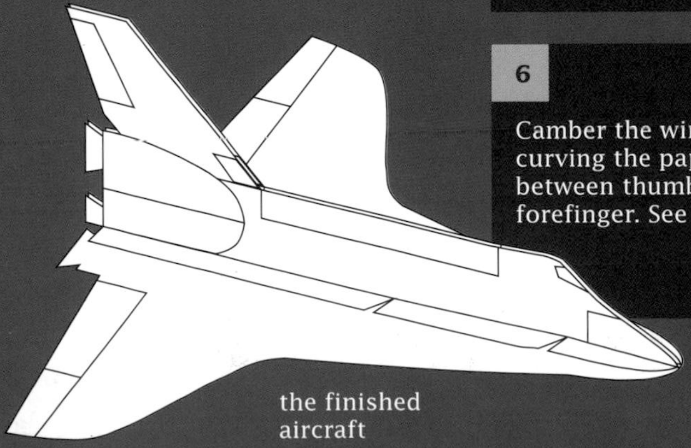

the finished aircraft

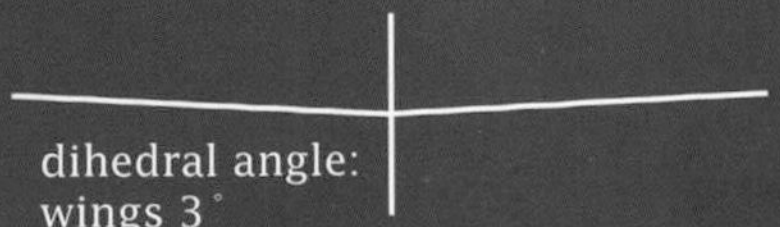

dihedral angle: wings 3°

camber: point of maximum camber 10% from front

- Cut on lines shown in black.
- Score lines in red.
- Use the blue lines as guides for adding details to the aircraft.
- ❯ Indicates the front edge of the piece.

NOTE: CUT OUT PHOTOCOPY ONLY

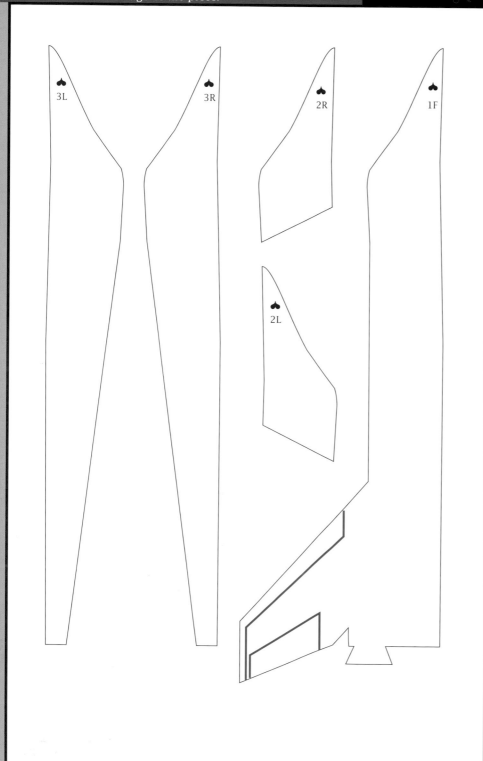

Space shuttle flights are commonplace today and we forget the incredible accomplishments of this machine. In April of 1981 the first Space Shuttle Orbiter lifted off the launch pad at Cape Canaveral, Florida, marking the beginning of a new era in space travel. Ever since the flights of the X-15 each venture into space required a completely new and expendable vehicle. The Shuttle was designed to be a service vehicle, going back and forth between earth and space, hence its name. Six have been built, which have been used variously to put a great many communications and observation satellites into orbit, as well as the Hubble telescope. Shuttles have been used for on-board experiments, to launch deep space vehicles on their way to other planets, and to recover previously delivered satellites for repairs. More recently they have delivered parts for the construction of the International Space Station.

Shuttle flight is spectacular. Launch takes about 8 minutes, from a vertical position, with the thrust for overcoming the forces of gravity and drag of the 4 million pound (1.8 million km) vehicle coming from two external, solid fuel booster rocket engines together with three liquid fuel rocket engines in the Shuttle itself. The boosters burn for 2 minutes, are jettisoned, and return to earth by

SPACE SHUTTLE PIECES

- Cut on lines shown in black.
- Score lines in red.
- Use the blue lines as guides for adding details to the aircraft.
- Indicates the front edge of the piece.

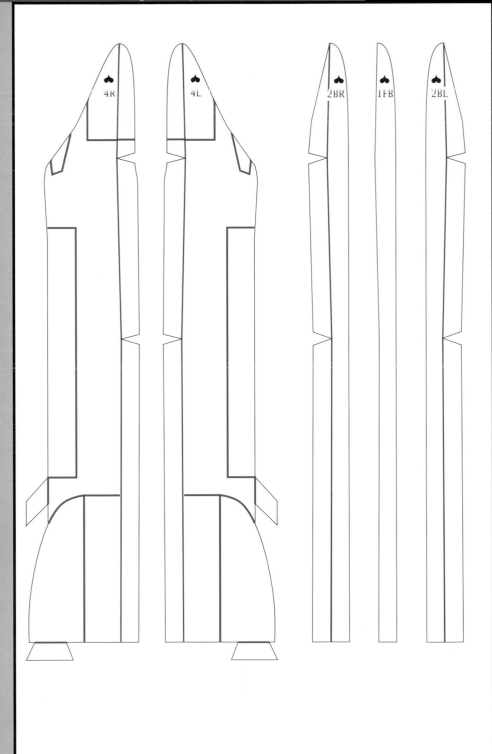

parachute while the other three engines burn for 8 minutes at which time the large external fuel tank, now empty, drops away and burns up as it plummets to earth. The Shuttle, by this time in space, traveling at a speed of over 17,000 mph (27,000 km/h) some 200 miles (320 km) up, fires its maneuvering engines to position it in earth orbit. While in space the sunward side is heated to 250 degrees F (120 degrees C) while the shade side is -250 degrees F. When its work in space is completed, the maneuvering engines are fired to reduce speed. The Shuttle descends through the atmosphere slowing down further by the force of drag which heats its skin to almost 3000 degrees F (1650 degrees C). Once at aerodynamic speed the Shuttle becomes a glider and is flown to a runway for landing.

AERONAUTICAL TERMS

Aspect ratio   The length of a wing in relation to its width. A square has an aspect ratio of 1.

Astronauts' wings   A qualification of pilots who go into space.

Ailerons   Surfaces on the trailing edges of wings that control roll.

Airfoil   A lift-generating surface; a wing.

Airframe   Those parts of an airplane (frame and skin surfaces) that give it the ability to fly.

Angle of attack   The downward slant, from front to back, of a wing to increase lift.

Attitude   The roll, pitch, and yaw of an aircraft in flight, and the direction it is pointing in relation to the horizon.

SPACE SHUTTLE PIECES

- Cut on lines shown in black.
- Score lines in red.
- Use the blue lines as guides for adding details to the aircraft.
- ✦ Indicates the front edge of the piece.

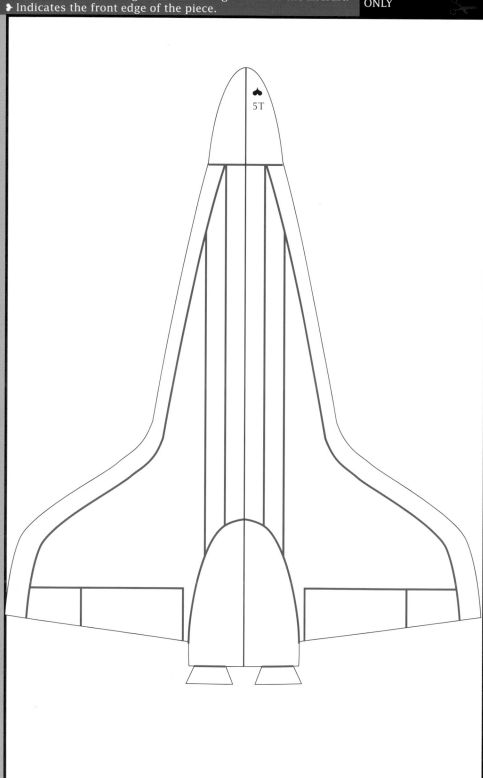

5T

Banking Raising the outside wing and lowering the inside wing during a turn.

Bird flight A bird's wing produces a lifting force near the bird's body where up and down motion is least and a propelling force with the large feathers at the tip where motion is greatest.

Canard airframe An airplane that has a small wing ahead of its main wing. The elevator, being ahead of the center of gravity, must be angled downward for flight.

Camber The convex curvature of the upper surface of a wing.

Center of gravity The point on an aircraft where its weight appears to be concentrated; its balancing point.

Center of lift The point on an aircraft where its lift appears to be concentrated.

Chord The measurement of a wing from front to back.

Control surfaces Small flat hinged surfaces on the trailing edges of wings and tail used to maintain equilibrium and maneuver an airplane.

Dihedral angle The upward slanting of wings away from the fuselage.

Dirigible A lighter-than-air powered, steerable aircraft, also called an airship.

Drag The resistance of air on moving objects.

Elevator Control surface on the trailing edge of the horizontal stabilizer used to control pitch.

Fly-by-wire Aircraft control surfaces that operate electronically rather than mechanically.

Fuselage The body of an airplane.

Gravity The force of the earth keeping objects on the ground and giving them weight.

High aspect ratio A wing that is very long in relation to its width.

Horizontal stabilizer A flat horizontal surface directs the flow of air in aid of maintaining equilibrium.

Hypersonic Speeds of between 5 and 7 times the speed of sound, 3700-5180 mph (5920-8288 km/h).

Internal combustion engine An engine in which mechanical energy is produced by the explosion of a mixture of fuel and air producing pressure on a piston in a cylinder.

Leading edge The front edge of an aircraft part.

Lift The force generated by the wings that counteracts the force of gravity.

Mach 1 The speed of sound, about 740 mph (1184 km/h).

Maneuver Skilfully making an airplane move in the correct manner and fly in the desired direction.

SPACE SHUTTLE PIECES

- Cut on lines shown in black.
- Score lines in red.
- Use the blue lines as guides for adding details to the aircraft.
- ↝ Indicates the front edge of the piece.

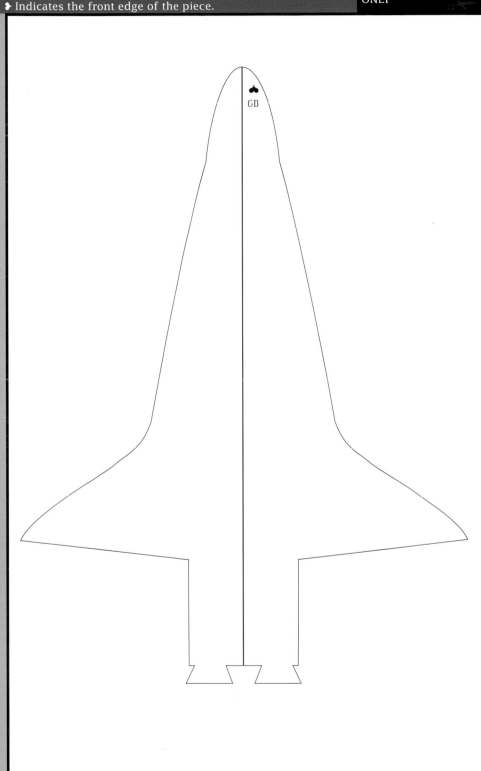

Pitch   The rotation of an airplane causing its nose to go up or down.

Roll   The rotation of an airplane causing the wingtips to rise or fall.

Rudder   Control surface on the trailing edge of the vertical stabilizer used to control yaw.

Shockwave   The pileup of sound waves around an object traveling at the speed of sound.

Sonic boom   The explosive sound of the shockwave being generated by an aircraft passing by at supersonic speed.

Sonic speed (sound barrier)   The speed at which sound waves move through the air.

Stall   The condition that occurs when a wing's angle of attack is too great.

Steam engine   An engine that produces mechanical energy by the pressure of steam produced outside the engine on a piston in a cylinder inside the engine.

Strakes   Small leading edge wing extensions at the wing root for added lift.

Streamlining   Shaping an airframe so that air flowing around it creates the least amount of drag.

Supercruise   An airplane flying at supersonic speed for an extended time.

Supersonic   The speed of an object greater than the speed of sound.

Thermal barrier   The amount of heat generated by drag that an airframe can withstand.

Thrust   The force needed to move an airplane forward.

Trailing edge   The back edge of an aircraft part.

Trim   The adjustment of control surfaces so that an airplane in flight does not roll, pitch, or yaw.

Vertical stabilizer   A flat vertical surface that directs the flow of air in aid of maintaining equilibrium.

Vortex   The air that swirls in a circular manner behind each wingtip as air slips from the high pressure area below to the low pressure area above.

Wing loading   The amount of weight a given area of wing is required to lift.

Wing span   The measurement from wingtip to wingtip.

Yaw   The rotation of an airplane causing its nose to go left or right.

INDEX